DIRTY MONEY EXPOSED

The Teen's Guide to Unmasking Financial Crimes

Ahmad M Sadeq

Disclaimer

The contents of this book are intended for educational purposes only. It should not be considered legal, financial, or professional advice. The author and publisher cannot be held responsible for any errors, omissions, or damages that may result from the use of the information provided. Additionally, any stories mentioned in this book are meant to be illustrative examples. These stories' characters, events, and scenarios are entirely fictional. Have been created to offer insights into concepts and topics discussed. Any similarities to individuals, whether entities or natural persons are purely coincidental and not intended to represent any specific individual, entity, or situation. The primary objective of these narratives is to promote understanding and engage readers in the matter.

To Fahad Aba AL Khail and Mo. Abu Swireh

I want to express my gratitude for your friendship. Your unwavering belief in me and the support you've provided have genuinely helped me achieve my goals. During times your steadfastness has been a source of hope and inspiration in my life. Our firm bond and my genuine appreciation towards you both cannot be understated. Thank you for going beyond not being friends but also as brothers.

With appreciation

Preface

Welcome to 'Dirty Money Exposed: The Teen's Guide to Unmasking Financial Crimes!' Why should you, a teen, care about this stuff? Simple: knowledge is power. This book will take you on a wild ride through the hidden world of financial trickery, from money laundering to fraud. We'll unmask the bad guys and see how their sneaky moves affect us all. You're not just reading for fun; you're gearing up to protect yourself and your future. So, let's dive in and turn you into a financial crime-fighting superhero. Ready?

Prologue

Welcome to "Dirty Money Exposed: The Teen's Guide to Unmasking Financial Crimes." Ever wondered about the shady side of money—the kind that cheats, steals, and ruins lives? You're not alone, and this book is your ticket into that hidden world.

Here's the deal: Money can either be a tool to help people or a weapon to harm them. We're diving into the eye-opening universe of financial crimes like money laundering, fraud, and insider trading. You'll get an insider look at both the villains behind these schemes and the heroes battling to stop them.

Why should you care? Because it's not just about dollars and cents. It's about fairness, integrity, and the world we're shaping for the future. Armed with knowledge, you can be part of the solution.

"Dirty Money Exposed" is not just a read; it's a ride—one that starts with your curiosity and ends with you empowered to make a difference, no matter your age. Ready to jump in?

Introduction

**THE BOOK OF LITTLE ABOUT EVERYTHING MATTERS
AND RELATED TO FINANCIAL CRIMES**

Hey there! Welcome to " Dirty Money Exposed: The Teens' Guide to Unmasking Financial Crimes." I'm excited to have you join us on this eye-opening adventure as we explore the realm of crimes and money laundering.

Money, they say, makes the world go round. What happens when it takes a turn and gets involved in fraud, corruption, and criminal activities? That's what we will uncover the side of finance, where hidden profits cause havoc in society.

You might wonder why a teenager like yourself should bother with the complexities of crimes. Well, here's the simple truth; knowledge is power. You can protect yourself and your future by understanding the world of crimes and how corrupt individuals operate. You'll also be better equipped to make an impact in a world that strives for integrity.

This book will provide an accessible overview of the foundations of crimes and money laundering. But that's not all! We'll also explore captivating stories that vividly illustrate these concepts. These narratives will help you grasp the essentials of crimes in an engaging and relatable way.

I aim to equip you with the knowledge and awareness needed to navigate the web of deception successfully. Together we have the power to cultivate a generation of well-informed, morally upright individuals prepared to stand united against the scourge of financial crimes. You may be curious about my motivation for addressing this subject.

Well, let me tell you that I'm not just an expert in this field; I am also a father, brother, son, friend—simply a human being. I intend to raise awareness beyond the realm of finance itself because financial crimes impact all of us regardless of backgrounds or aspirations.

As a someone with expertise in this domain, I have observed a pattern of escalating crime rates on a scale despite various preventive measures being taken. However, amidst these concerns lies something you—the youth—representing a glimmer of hope! By gaining an understanding of crimes and developing strategies to combat them, you possess the potential to become catalysts for positive transformation in our world.

Imagine living in a society where criminals effortlessly exploit the system's intricacies while innocent individuals bear the brunt of their actions. We can no longer turn an eye to this underworld. By comprehending money laundering techniques and unravelling the methods employed by individuals, we can shield ourselves and our communities from harm.

Rest assured that this book will not leave you feeling terrified or helpless. On the contrary, it aims to equip you with knowledge and skills that will enable you to identify, comprehend and effectively counteract crimes. We will dispel myths surrounding these issues. Expose the tactics employed by those seeking to conceal their gotten gains.

Prepare yourself for a journey as we uncover the mysteries

behind crimes and equip you with the tools to make a meaningful impact. Together let's take on this challenge and work towards building a more financial world.

As you delve into this book, you may encounter instances where specific points and discussions are repeated. This intentional repetition serves a purpose; it underscores the importance of concepts that deserve attention.

THE ROAD MAP

The book is divided into five sections Consist of thirteen chapters and Stories Section, followed by "Final Message." here is the road map.

Section One: The Crime

This enlightening section comprising two chapters, delves into the truths surrounding activities, money laundering, and criminal behaviour. We also discuss the importance of literacy for teenagers and how they can safeguard themselves and their future against exploitation.

Chapter 1: The Unmasking

This chapter sets the groundwork for the book. We explore forms of financial activities, their driving forces, and the individuals or groups involved. We can gain insights into their impact by understanding what contributes to these practices. Develop more effective strategies to combat them.

Chapter 2: The Concern

We examine how financial crimes deeply affect teenagers, communities, and economies. These crimes undermine our trust in the system's reliability. Consequently, this chapter empowers teenagers to make decisions by identifying risks and taking precautions to protect themselves. It equips them with tools to navigate a world of financial crimes and build a more secure future. Always remember that combating crimes requires cooperation. You can make a difference beyond your circle of friends by educating your peers,

engaging in discussions, and advocating for ethical money management.
Together we can build a future where financial crimes are exposed and thwarted.

Section Two: The Escape

This section, comprising five chapters, will provide insights into transforming money. You'll learn about criminal activities and the diverse methods and pathways criminals employ to hide their illegal gains. Discover why criminals resort to money laundering and how you can contribute to the fight against it by recognizing transactions and understanding the process of cleaning illicit funds.

Chapter 3: The Laundry

By comprehending the intricacies of money laundering, you'll become more attuned to activities and better equipped to identify and prevent them.

Chapter 4: The Need for Laundering

This chapter will explore the agendas behind money laundering and its crucial role in hiding profits. We will delve into the methods used by criminals to cleanse their gotten gains and avoid detection.

Chapter 5: The Terrorist Financing

This chapter sheds light on terrorism, uncovering the financial support network that fuels these perilous activities. Discover the connections between financing terrorism and money laundering and understand their differences. And appreciate the importance of combating financing in safeguarding global security.

Chapter 6: The Funnels and Channels

You will venture into both underground avenues for money laundering and funding terrorism. Explore the channels that enable funds to flow undetected while uncovering various techniques employed in money laundering and terrorist financing. Unravel the complexities behind these operations as we illuminate their mechanisms.

Section Three: The Impact

In this section, we will examine how these crimes do not affect stability but also have profound emotional consequences. Our journey will also take us into norms and global repercussions revealing how financial crime weaves a web.

Chapter 7: The Economic Implications

In this chapter, our focus will be on exploring the implications arising from financial crimes. These crimes have reaching effects beyond numbers on a financial statement. They disrupt productivity, widen the gap between the rich and the poor, and discourage investments. This analysis will examine how these crimes contribute to imbalances that impact communities and nations in real-life scenarios.

Chapter 8: The Psychological Implications

Moving on to the chapter, we will delve into the consequences of financial crimes for individuals and societies.
Apart from causing losses, these crimes erode trust, instil fear and shake people's belief in established systems. Understanding the aftermath will shed light on the scars left by financial crimes.

Chapter 9: The Social and Cultural Implications

This chapter takes us through the cultural implications of crimes. We will explore how these offenses can reshape norms and cultural values by unravelling community bonds and normalizing corrupt behaviour. It serves as a reminder that financial crimes are not isolated incidents but are intricately woven into our collective identity.

Chapter 10: The Global Impact

As we advance to this chapter, our focus expands to examine the global consequences of financial crimes. The impact of crimes is extensive, affecting not only the global economy but also giving rise to transnational criminal networks and undermining the institutions that exist to safeguard our world. This perspective will connect the dots between incidents and their broader global implications.

Section Four: The Fight

In this section, you will not gain knowledge on combating crimes but also acquire skills to protect yourself from scams and exploitation. I will guide you in recognizing warning signs and what actions to take if you come across one.

Additionally, we will explore career opportunities such as compliance officers, forensic accountants, and financial investigators, where your expertise can be used to combat crimes. We will also discuss efforts that play a role in fighting these crimes globally. So, prepare yourself to embrace your role as a guardian of integrity and explore ways to make the financial world safer.

Chapter 11: The Right Reaction

You will learn steps to follow when faced with warning signs or illegal financial activities. Discover how to respond, seek assistance from trusted adults, and report incidents to the relevant authorities.

Chapter 12: The Roles and Jobs

This chapter will delve into your teenage role and how you can actively contribute to the fight against financial crimes. We'll explore opportunities and skills that can make a difference even at this stage of your life. Additionally, we'll discuss roles in financial crime prevention, such as compliance officers, forensic accountants, and financial investigators. Understanding these career paths can pave the way for an impactful future in combating crimes.

Chapter 13: The Unity

In this chapter, we will take a perspective on combating financial activities. We'll learn about the efforts between countries and international organizations to tackle crimes

and money laundering. Discover how the world is coming together to create a more secure environment that benefits everyone's prosperity. But before we dive in, let us understand why teenagers may be attracted to criminal activities or groups.

Section Five: Story Time

In this last section, we'll explore a series of fictional stories crafted to take you on an exciting adventure through the complex world of financial crimes and ethics.

Contents

CHANNELS

A – Z
Glossary

Glossary & Key Notes

Navigating the world of financial crimes and criminology can sometimes feel like deciphering a secret code. Words, terms, and expressions pop up that might seem unfamiliar or even mysterious. It's a world filled with concepts that are not only fascinating but also deeply significant in understanding how crimes, especially financial ones, take shape in our society. But fear not! This glossary is here to be your guide; This glossary covers more than 120 definitions.

I believe that understanding doesn't have to be a mountainous task. Knowledge should be accessible and engaging, not hidden behind complex jargon. That's why I've put together this glossary—to break down the barriers and make the information in this book as clear and understandable as possible.

In this Glossary, you'll find simple explanations for some of the terms and concepts that appear throughout the book and others were not mentioned but related. I've taken care to define them in a way that's easy to grasp, even if you're new to this field. Think of it as a handy roadmap to help you navigate the intricate pathways of financial crimes and criminology.

Whether you're a curious beginner or someone keen to delve deeper into this world, this glossary is designed to support your journey. Feel free to jump back to this section whenever you come across a word or idea that's new to you. Or simply browse through it to explore and learn something new. Remember, knowledge is power, and understanding these terms is like holding a key to unlock a deeper awareness of the world around us. Happy exploring!

A

Anomie: A state of normlessness where social norms are confused, unclear, or absent, often leading to a breakdown in social cohesiveness.

Anti-Money Laundering (AML): Rules and procedures to prevent criminals from hiding the illegal origins of their money by making it look like it came from legal sources.

Asset Forfeiture: The legal seizure of assets that have been involved in criminal activities.

Asset Management: The process of managing a client's investments, including buying, selling, and monitoring assets.

B

Bank Fraud: Engaging in a scheme to defraud a bank or using deceptive practices to secure funds or credits from a bank.

Bankruptcy: A legal state where an individual or organization cannot repay debts owed to creditors.

Behaviorism: A psychological approach that emphasizes observable behaviors over thoughts or feelings.

Black Market: An illegal market where goods or services are bought and sold without government regulation.

Bonds: A type of fixed-income investment, essentially a loan to a corporation or government, which pays interest to the bondholder.

Bribery: Offering, giving, or receiving something valuable, like money or gifts, to influence someone's actions in an illegal or unethical way.

Bull Market: A market characterized by rising prices for securities, indicating investor confidence.

C

Capital Markets: Financial markets that facilitate the buying and selling of long-term debt and equity instruments.

Central Bank: A governmental or quasi-governmental organization that manages a country's money supply, interest rates, and overall financial stability.

Classical Criminology: A school of thought focusing on the assumption that individuals choose to commit crimes after weighing the benefits and drawbacks.

Cognitive Dissonance: A psychological state where conflicting attitudes, beliefs, or behaviors cause mental discomfort.

Collective Behavior: The action or behavior of people in groups or crowds, often unpredictable and sometimes associated with criminal behavior.

Commercial Banking: Banking services provided to businesses, including loans, credit, and deposit accounts.

Commodities: Basic goods used in commerce, such as metals, agricultural products, and energy resources, that are interchangeable with other goods of the same type.

Compliance: Following laws and regulations, often related to financial activities to prevent illegal or unethical behavior.

Compound Interest: Interest calculated on the initial principal as well as on the accumulated interest from previous periods.

Conflict Theory: A sociological perspective that emphasizes social inequalities, often applied to understand the relationship between law, crime, and inequality.

Conformity: Adjusting attitudes or behaviors to align with social norms or pressures.

Control Theory: In criminology, the idea that people would act out without social controls or constraints, emphasizing the structures that keep individuals in line.

Counterfeit: Making an imitation of something, usually money or branded products, with the intent to deceive or defraud.

Credit Card Fraud: Illegally using someone else's credit card information to buy things or steal money.

Credit Rating: An assessment of a borrower's ability to repay debt, often assigned by credit rating agencies.

Cryptocurrency: A type of digital currency that relies on cryptography for security and operates independently of a central bank.

Criminogenesis: The origins or causes of criminal behavior.

Cultural Relativism: The idea that beliefs and activities should be understood within the context of the individual's own culture, often in opposition to ethnocentrism.

Cybercrime: Crimes that happen online, such as hacking or online scams.

D

Deviance: Behaviors or actions that violate social norms, which may or may not be criminal.

Derivatives: Financial contracts whose value is derived from underlying assets, such as stocks, bonds, or commodities.

Deterrence Theory: The concept in criminology that punishment should deter individuals from committing future crimes.

Dividends: Payments made by a corporation to its shareholders, usually from profits.

Due Diligence: The process of investigating and verifying the details of a potential investment, business agreement, or other financial deal to identify risks.

E

Embezzlement: Taking money that you were trusted to manage (like in a company) for your personal use without permission.

Enhanced Due Diligence (EDD): A more detailed form of due diligence conducted on higher-risk customers to understand their background, financial dealings, and to mitigate risks.

Equity: Ownership interest in a corporation, typically represented by shares of stock.

Ethnocentrism: Judging other cultures by the standards of one's own culture, often leading to misunderstandings or biases.

Exchange Rate: The value of one currency in terms of another currency.

Extortion: Forcing someone to give you money, property, or favors by threatening harm or exposing secrets.

F

Financial Intelligence Unit (FIU): A government agency responsible for receiving, analyzing, and transmitting disclosures on suspicious or unusual financial activity related to money laundering and terrorist financing.

Fiscal Policy: Government policy related to taxing and spending to influence the economy.

Foreign Exchange (Forex) Market: The market in which currencies are traded globally.

Forensic Psychology: The intersection of psychology and law, including the psychological assessment of those involved in legal cases.

Forgery: Creating, altering, or using a false document with

the intent to deceive or defraud.

Fraud: Tricking someone for personal gain, often involving deception or false representation.

Fundamental Analysis: Assessing the intrinsic value of a security by examining financial and economic factors.

G

GDP (Gross Domestic Product): The total value of all goods and services produced within a country in a specific time period.

Globalization: The process of increasing interconnection and interdependence of the world's markets and businesses.

Greed Theory: A theory that attributes criminal behavior to excessive desire for material wealth or possessions, leading to unethical or illegal activities.

H

Habeas Corpus: A legal principle that protects individuals from unlawful detention or imprisonment.

Hedging: Using financial instruments or investments to offset potential losses or gains in another investment.

Hedge Funds: Investment funds that use aggressive strategies to achieve high returns, often using leverage, short-selling, and derivatives.

Human Capital: The skills, knowledge, and abilities possessed by individuals, seen as valuable resources for economic development.

I

Identity Theft: Stealing someone else's personal information to impersonate them, usually for financial gain.

Ideology: A set of beliefs, values, and opinions that shapes the way a person or a group views the world.

Inflation: The general rise in prices across an economy,

decreasing the purchasing power of money.

Insider Trading: Buying or selling stocks based on confidential information, illegal in many jurisdictions.

Insurance Fraud: Falsifying information to obtain insurance benefits or staging accidents to collect insurance money.

Interest Rate: The amount charged by a lender to a borrower for the use of money, usually expressed as an annual percentage.

Investment Banking: Banking services that help companies raise capital, manage mergers and acquisitions, and provide other financial guidance.

J

Joint Venture: A business agreement between two or more parties to work together on a specific project or business activity, sharing profits, losses, and governance.

K

Keynesian Economics: An economic theory emphasizing government intervention in the economy to manage demand and keep unemployment low.

Know Your Customer (KYC): A business process used to verify the identity of clients, aiming to prevent identity theft, financial fraud, money laundering, and terrorist financing.

L

Labor Market: The supply and demand for labor, where employers seek to hire workers, and individuals look for employment.

Laissez-faire Economics: An economic philosophy that opposes government intervention in the marketplace.

Liability: A legal obligation to pay debts or fulfill other responsibilities.

Liberalism: A political and moral philosophy based on

liberty, consent of the governed, and equality before the law.

Liquidity: The ease with which an asset can be converted into cash without affecting its market price.

Loan Sharking: Lending money at extremely high-interest rates and using threats or violence to collect the debt.

Long-Con: It refers to a scam or scheme that takes a long time to unfold. Unlike a "short con," which might take only a few minutes or hours to pull off, a long con requires more planning, time, and patience.

Long-Term Investment: Investments held for an extended period, typically more than a year.

M

Macroeconomics: The study of the economy as a whole, including factors like growth, inflation, unemployment, and fiscal and monetary policies.

Market Economy: An economic system where decisions about production, investment, and distribution are guided by the price signals created by the forces of supply and demand.

Mergers and Acquisitions (M&A): The consolidation of companies or assets through various types of financial transactions.

Microeconomics: The study of individual consumers, businesses, or markets, as opposed to the economy as a whole.

Monetary Policy: The management of a country's money supply and interest rates by its central bank to control inflation and stabilize the currency.

Money Laundering: The process of making illegally-gained money appear legal by hiding its origins.

Mortgage Fraud: Misleading or lying about information on a mortgage application to obtain a loan or larger loan amount.

Mutual Funds: Investment funds that pool money from many investors to buy a diversified portfolio of stocks, bonds, or other securities.

Money Mule: A money mule is someone who moves stolen money through their bank account, often without knowing that it's illegal. Think of it like carrying a bag of money for a stranger without knowing where it came from; it might seem harmless, but it can get you in trouble with the law.

N

Narcoterrorism: Terrorism associated with trade in illicit drugs.

Neoclassical Economics: An economic approach emphasizing rational individuals and efficient markets, often focusing on supply and demand.

Non-Governmental Organization (NGO): Private organizations that operate without government intervention, often focused on social, environmental, or humanitarian objectives.

O

Oligopoly: A market structure where a small number of firms have the majority of market share, often leading to less competition and higher prices.

Organized Crime: Criminal activities carried out by structured groups, like the mafia or drug cartels, often involved in illegal business ventures.

P

Ponzi Scheme: A fraudulent investment scheme where returns are paid to earlier investors from the capital of newer investors, rather than from profit.

Portfolio: A collection of financial investments, like stocks, bonds, or other assets, owned by an individual or organization.

Positivist Criminology: A branch of criminology that emphasizes the understanding of criminal behavior through scientific methods and objective evidence.

Predatory Lending: Unfair or deceptive lending practices that take advantage of borrowers, often involving high interest rates or hidden fees.

Price Manipulation: Unlawful actions to artificially inflate or deflate the price of a security or commodity.

Privatization: The transfer of ownership or operation of public assets, services, or industries to private ownership.

Probation: A legal status where an offender is allowed to remain in the community under supervision instead of serving time in prison.

Psychological Profiling: The process of using behavioral and psychological characteristics to identify potential criminal suspects.

Public Policy: Government actions, including laws, regulations, and funding priorities, intended to achieve specific societal goals.

Pump-and-Dump: A fraudulent investment scheme where promoters artificially inflate the price of a stock, sell their shares, and then let the price crash.

Q

Quantitative Easing (QE): A non-traditional monetary policy where a central bank purchases government securities to increase the money supply and lower interest rates.

R

Racketeering: Operating illegal businesses or schemes to make a profit, often associated with organized crime.

Rational Choice Theory: The idea in economics and sociology that individuals make decisions based on rational calculations of the costs and benefits.

Recession: A period of reduced economic activity, often defined as two consecutive quarters of negative GDP growth.

Regulation: Government rules or laws that control or oversee business practices to protect public interests or achieve policy goals.

Regulatory Compliance: The adherence to laws, regulations, guidelines, and specifications relevant to specific industries or sectors.

Risk Assessment: The process of identifying and analyzing potential issues that could negatively impact an organization, particularly regarding finance and reputation.

Risk-Based Approach (RBA): An approach that involves assessing the risks related to money laundering, terrorist financing, and other related threats and then applying appropriate measures to manage and mitigate those risks.

Risk Management: Identifying, assessing, and controlling threats to an organization's capital and earnings.

RICO Act: The Racketeer Influenced and Corrupt Organizations Act, a U.S. law aimed at fighting organized crime.

S

Sanctions: Penalties or restrictions imposed by governments to enforce international law, often related to international politics and economics.

Securities: Financial instruments, like stocks and bonds, representing ownership, a debt agreement, or rights to ownership.

Short Con: It is like the quicker, sneakier cousin of the long con. It's a scam that's pulled off quickly, usually in a matter of minutes or even seconds, without the need for an elaborate plan or deep trust with the victim.

Social Contract Theory: A philosophical idea that people live together in society by mutual consent to form rules and create a government.

Social Disorganization Theory: A criminological theory that attributes crime to the breakdown of community institutions, relationships, and social controls.

Social Learning Theory: A psychological theory suggesting that people learn from one another through observation, imitation, and modeling.

Speculation: Investment in assets or financial instruments with high risk, hoping to profit from short-term price fluctuations.

Stock Market: A place where shares of publicly-traded companies are bought and sold.

Strain Theory: A sociological perspective that sees crime as a response to the disconnect between cultural goals and the means to achieve them.

Subprime Mortgage: A type of mortgage offered to homebuyers with poor credit, often having higher interest rates and less favorable terms.

Supply Chain: The network of individuals, organizations, resources, and processes involved in creating and selling a product or service.

Suspicious Activity Report (SAR): A document that financial institutions must file with the FIU if they suspect any fraudulent activities or transactions that may involve money laundering or fraud.

Syndicate: A group of individuals or organizations that work together to achieve a common goal, often used to refer to organized crime groups.

T

Tariff: A tax on imported or exported goods.

Tax Evasion: Illegally avoiding paying taxes, often by underreporting income or inflating deductions.

Technical Analysis: Examining statistical trends from trading activity to predict future price movements in financial markets.

Terrorism: The use of violence or threats to intimidate or coerce, especially for political purposes.

Tort Law: Legal principles governing civil wrongs, where one party's behavior causes harm or loss to another.

Trade Union: An organization of workers who join together to achieve common goals, such as better working conditions or wages.

Transparency: Openness and honesty in communication, decision-making, and operations, often seen as a sign of good governance.

U

Unemployment: The state of being without a paid job but available to work.

Usury: The illegal practice of lending money at extremely high-interest rates.

V

Venture Capital: Financing provided to start-up companies in exchange for equity, often in industries with high growth potential.

Victimology: The study of victims, including their relationships with offenders, their experiences with the criminal justice system, and the social impacts of crime.

W

White-Collar Crime: Non-violent crimes committed by individuals or organizations in business activities, often involving fraud or financial manipulation.

Whistleblower: An individual who exposes wrongdoing or illegal activities within an organization.

Whistleblowing: The act of exposing wrongdoing or unethical behavior within an organization, often related to financial malpractice or fraud.

WTO (World Trade Organization): An international organization that regulates trade between nations, aiming to ensure that trade flows smoothly and predictably.

Y

Yield: The income earned from an investment, usually expressed as a percentage of the investment's cost or current market value.

Z

Zero-Sum Game: A situation in economics or game theory where one participant's gain or loss is exactly balanced by the losses or gains of other participants.

Key Notes

Some of the terms you'll encounter in this book may seem complex at first glance. To help you dive into the subject matter and fully engage with the content, I've provided detailed explanations for specific words and phrases. These elaborations will guide you as you read, making it easier to understand the intricate world of financial crimes:

- An economy can be seen as a system encompassing the processes of earning, spending, and exchanging money. It also delves into how individuals secure employment opportunities and generate income.

- Insider trading refers to when someone exploits concealed knowledge to engage in buying or selling stocks or other investments granting them an advantage over others.

- Ponzi scams occur when individuals promise returns on investments but instead utilize funds from new investors to pay off earlier ones instead of generating actual profits.

Eventually this scheme unravels, resulting in losses, for many people involved.

- Accounting fraud is when companies change their financial records to make their income or financial health look better than they are. This can confuse investors and make the company and the business less stable.

- An Ideology refers to a set of beliefs, ideas, values, and principles that form the foundation of a particular social, political, or economic system. It encompasses a comprehensive worldview and provides a framework for understanding and interpreting the world. Ideologies guide individuals' perceptions, attitudes, and behaviours, shaping their understanding of society, morality, governance, and power distribution.

- Ideological systems, on the other hand, are complex frameworks that encompass a collection of interconnected ideologies. They provide a comprehensive and structured approach to organising and governing various aspects of society. Ideological systems often include economic, political, social, and cultural dimensions to shape how individuals and communities function and interact.

- Ideological systems can vary widely, ranging from liberalism, conservatism, and socialism in the political sphere to capitalism, communism, and mixed economies in the economic sphere. Each system has its principles, goals, and strategies for addressing societal challenges and achieving desirable outcomes.

- Consumption (or " consumerism") mindsets value getting and using things for happiness, satisfaction, and social status. It's the idea that buying and owning things is life's most essential and a good measure of success. Consumerists value getting more things and see their self-worth and identity in their ability to get and show off these things. Advertising, social pressures, and the belief that buying and consuming more makes people happier and more satisfied cause this mindset. However, it can lead to overspending, debt, and a never-ending desire for more, detracting from relationships, experiences, and personal health.

- Materialistic psychology examines how focusing on things and money affects our thoughts, feelings, and acts. It looks at how wanting things can affect our happiness, self-esteem, and relationships with other people. It also examines the reasons behind our materialistic behaviours and the potential negative consequences of excessive materialism.

- Motivation is the inner drive or incentive that drives an individual to act in a certain way or pursue a specific goal. The underlying reason or purpose drives and directs behaviour. Motivation can be intrinsic (driven by personal desires or values) or extrinsic (influenced by external rewards or consequences).

- Root cause and motivation are related but frequently interchangeable concepts. The root cause is the fundamental underlying reason or source that leads to a specific problem or issue. The initial event starts a chain of events that results in a specific outcome or behaviour. Understanding the deeper factors contributing to a problem is critical for identifying the root cause, as addressing the root cause can help prevent the issue from recurring. On the other hand, motivation is the inner drive or incentive that drives an individual to act in a certain way or pursue a specific goal. The underlying reason or purpose drives and directs behaviour.

- Individuals who have become corrupt are capable of manipulating and deceiving others via the use of charm and persuasion in order to accomplish their own self-serving aims while ignoring the negative effects of their actions.

- Cynicism is when someone has a hard time believing that people are genuinely good or that they do things for the right reasons. They often think that others are being sneaky or selfish. It's like having a doubt in people's kindness and honesty.

The Cheat Sheet

Follow the outlined reading plan diligently, and I assure you that within 30 days, you'll emerge as a more informed and empowered teenager.

Welcome to the guided reading plan for "Dirty Money Exposed." This plan is designed to help you navigate through the chapters and gain a comprehensive understanding of the complexities of financial crimes, their impact, and the actions to combat them.

By dedicating 30–60 minutes per day and engaging in 15 minutes of extended self-research, you'll uncover insights that empower you to make informed decisions and contribute to a safer financial landscape.

Day 1-5: Chapter 1 "The Unmasking"

Begin your journey by laying the groundwork. Explore different forms of financial activities, their driving forces, and the individuals or groups involved. Delve into the intricate world of financial practices to understand their motives.

Day 6-7: Chapter 2 "The Concern"

Dive into the impact of financial crimes on individuals, communities, and economies. Learn how these crimes erode trust in systems and empower yourself by identifying risks and taking precautions. Equip yourself with tools to navigate a world of financial crimes and build a more secure future.

Day 8–9: Chapter 3 "The Laundry"

Comprehend the intricacies of money laundering. Develop a keen sense of its associated activities, enabling you to identify and prevent these illicit actions.

Day 10-11: Chapter 4 "The Need for Laundering"

Explore the agendas behind money laundering and its crucial role in hiding profits. Uncover methods used by criminals to cleanse their ill-gotten gains and evade detection.

Day 12-13: Chapter 5 "The Terrorist Financing"

Shed light on the realm of terrorism financing. Understand the network of financial support fueling these perilous activities. Gain insights into the connections between financing terrorism and money laundering.

Day 14–15: Chapter 6 "The Funnels and Channels"

Venture into underground avenues used for money laundering and funding terrorism. Explore the channels enabling undetected fund flow, uncovering techniques employed in money laundering and terrorist financing operations.

Day 16–17: Chapter 7 "The Economic Implications"

Dive into the far-reaching economic repercussions of financial crimes. Explore how these crimes disrupt productivity, amplify disparities, and discourage investments. Understand how these imbalances impact communities and nations in real-life scenarios.

Day 18-19: Chapter 8 "The Psychological Implications"

Navigate the emotional aftermath of financial crimes for individuals and societies. Discover how these crimes erode trust, instil fear, and shake faith in established systems, leaving lasting scars.

Day 20–21: Chapter 9 "The Social and Cultural Implications"

Explore the cultural impact of financial crimes. Understand how these offenses reshape norms and values, impacting communities and normalizing corrupt behaviour.

Day 22-23: Chapter 10 "The Global Impact"

Grasp the extensive consequences of financial crimes on a global scale. Understand their effects on economies, transnational networks, and institutions safeguarding our world.

Day 24-25: Chapter 11 "The Right Reaction"

Learn the steps to follow when faced with warning signs or illegal financial activities. Discover how to respond, seek assistance from trusted adults, and report incidents to relevant authorities.

Day 26–27: Chapter 12 "The Roles and Jobs"

Delve into your role as a teenager in combating financial crimes. Explore opportunities, skills to make a difference, and functions like compliance officers, forensic accountants, and financial investigators.

Day 28-29: Chapter 13 "The Unity"

Learn about global efforts, collaborations, and international organizations fighting financial crimes. Discover how the world is uniting to create a secure environment for prosperity.

Day 30: Section Five "Story Time"

This is a thrilling and eye-opening part of our journey! In this section, you'll find over 30 fictional yet incredibly realistic stories, each one a vivid window into the world where teens like you might encounter financial crimes. Congratulations! You've completed the guided reading plan. By dedicating focused time to each chapter and engaging in self-research, you've gained valuable insights to navigate the world of financial crimes and contribute to a safer economic landscape.

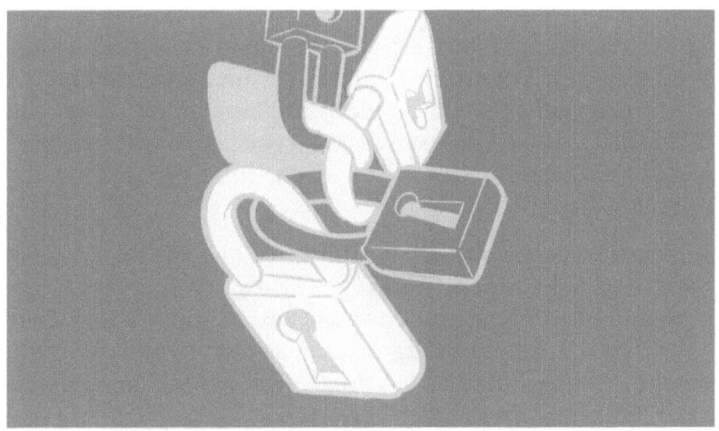

Teens' Secrets & Apathy

I t is natural for teenagers to desire freedom and privacy as they become more independent. They may feel confident in their abilities, and believe they can handle everything on their own. However, teens must recognize the dangers of keeping secrets and isolating themselves. Here I will discuss why teenagers might choose to hide information from their parents:

- The Desire for Independence; During their teenage years, youths undergo a phase of self-discovery where they strive to establish their identity and assert independence. They may wish to make decisions, handle challenges independently, and explore experiences. While this is a part of growing up, it can lead teens to hide aspects of their lives from their parents.

- Teenagers often worry that they will face judgment: from their parents regarding their choices, interests, or mistakes. Due to this fear, they might conceal parts of their lives to avoid conflict or disappointment. They may believe they possess all the knowledge and capability when they require important insights or additional experience.

- Pushing Boundaries: As teenagers navigate self-discovery, they may test boundaries to gauge limits and understand the consequences of engaging in behaviour. This can make them secretive because they venture into territories with knowledge, sometimes without fully recognizing the potential risks.

- Lack of awareness: Teenagers, due to their life experiences compared to adults, may not fully comprehend the consequences of their actions. They might believe they possess an understanding of subjects or situations. As a result, they might make decisions without seeking guidance or assistance from adults.

HOWEVER, TEENAGERS MUST UNDERSTAND THE DRAWBACKS OF KEEPING SECRETS FROM THEIR PARENTS. SOME OF THESE RISKS INCLUDE:

- Vulnerability to exploitation: Teens who keep secrets may be more susceptible to manipulation or exploitation by peers, online predators, or individuals with intentions.

- Lack of Support: By confiding in their parents, teenagers can benefit from advice, support, and insights gained through life experiences that can assist them. Being secretive will surely lead to losing such valuable support.

BUT WHY CRIMINALS WOULD TARGET TEENAGERS? THIS A FREQUENT QUESTION TEENS AND THIER PARENTS ASK; HERE ARE A FEW REASONS WHY:

- Lack of experience: Teenagers often have limited knowledge about money management, personal safety practices, and online activities due to their lack of exposure; Criminals take advantage of this lack of experience to deceive and manipulate them.

- Teenagers tend to be trusting, which can make them susceptible to manipulation. Criminals exploit this trust by obtaining information or bank account details or by persuading teenagers to engage in activities unknowingly.

- Teenagers often need money or access, making them vulnerable to offers that promise easy ways to earn. Criminals might exploit them as "money mules" for laundering illicit funds and involve them in scams.

- Social media and online presence play a role in the lives of teenagers because sometimes they share excessive personal information online. Criminals capitalize on this by employing social engineering tactics to extract details, steal identities or deceive teenagers into falling for scams.

- Peer pressure: this is another factor among teenagers. They may feel compelled to engage in illegal activities to fit in or gain acceptance. Criminals take advantage of this vulnerability by coaxing them into participating in drug sales, shoplifting, or other unlawful behaviour.

- The lack of knowledge also makes teenagers susceptible to exploitation. They may need awareness about the risks and consequences of actions such as sharing information online, making illegal purchases, or engaging in money laundering schemes. We will discuss this topic later in the book.

Growing The Right Apathy

In emotions and mindsets, apathy is vital; it signifies a state in which an individual experiences a lack of interest, enthusiasm, or concern toward certain aspects of life.

However, it's important to note that apathy is not a one-size-fits-all concept. It encompasses states, each with its unique characteristics and implications. This book takes inspiration from three aspects of apathy: the positive, the negative, and the ugly. While I won't go into detail about these definitions, their influence can be subtly seen throughout the pages.

The discussions and stories within the chapters reflect the complexities of behaviour, the consequences of apathy, and the power of acting. As you navigate through the chapters and discussions on crimes and their wide-ranging impacts, you must consider the various shades of apathy and how they interact with the shared stories here.

Remember that your awareness and empathy can counteract apathy and help create a society that opposes exploitation while embracing accountability.

Definition 1: Good Apathy refers to a state of mind where individuals actively rebel against any factors that could harm themselves or others. It is not disinteresting but rather an active rejection of negative influences. Individuals experiencing Good Apathy possess heightened awareness. They prioritize their well-being and others by making choices that promote positivity and contribute to creating a world.

Definition 2: Bad Apathy represents a form of apathy where individuals lose motivation feel lack confidence.

In this state, people might start not caring about things that could harm their plans or well-being. They may need to focus on their responsibilities, disregard warning signs, and fail to take measures. Bad Apathy arises from a feeling of helplessness. It can hinder growth and success if left unaddressed.

Definition 3: Ugly Apathy is characterized by a self-centred mindset where individuals prioritize their benefits and desires without considering the well-being of others. It is a state of indifference where people disconnect from the consequences of their actions disregarding how they affect others. This can lead to a lack of empathy and neglect for the good. Recognizing and addressing this mentality is crucial in promoting a compassionate and connected society. My Theory "Advancing Backwards" proposes that people can move towards Good Apathy by acknowledging and dealing with the aspects of Bad and Ugly Apathy. It highlights the significance of self-reflection, self-awareness, and conscious decision-making. By reflecting on themselves, individuals can identify signs of Bad and Ugly within them. Take steps to overcome these states. According to the theory, personal development and positive transformation happen when individuals actively choose not to embrace characteristics and instead focus on creating a meaningful and purposeful direction in life. In this book, we will address the issue of crimes as they impact others and our lives.

In Pursuit of Financial Freedom, We Embrace Knowledge to Outmaneuver Financial Crimes and Unleash Our Good Greed, Apathy & Incompetence.

AHMAD M SADEQ

SECTION ONE:
THE CRIME

In this section, you will understand financial crimes and their implications comprehensively in this section. The three key chapters delve into illicit financial activities, highlighting the types of crimes, their motivations, and the individuals involved.

Readers also explore the profound effects of financial crimes on teenagers, communities, and economies, empowering them to make informed decisions and navigate the complex financial landscape.

And it concludes by emphasizing individual responsibility in preventing financial crimes and promoting ethical behaviour, equipping readers with the knowledge, awareness, and strategies to actively contribute to a future where financial crimes are exposed and prevented.

CHAPTER ONE: THE UNMASKING

This chapter is essential because it lays the groundwork for the rest of the book. We are going to investigate the various forms of illegal financial activity, the motivations that lie behind them, as well as the individuals and organizations that are involved.

Suppose we have a better understanding of the factors that contribute to the existence of these illegal activities. In that case, we will be able to develop more effective strategies to combat them and have a better understanding of the effects those activities have. Also, we will embark on a journey through the world of lucrative criminal enterprises and unveil the secrets behind ventures that yield financial rewards.

THE SHADES

Financial crimes may seem to have nothing to do with a teenager's life, but on the contrary, they considerably affect our society and teen future. "The Shades" discusses the definition of financial crimes, how they started, and their modern setup. Understanding these topics is essential to unveil the dark side of dirty money to protect yourself, make good decisions, and help make the financial system more open and fairer.

The Definition & Birth Of Financial Crimes

Let us start with the simplified definition of Financial Crime, which refers to unethical actions that involve misleading and defrauding others for one's financial gain. It involves, for example, deceiving people into disclosing their personal information, fraud, scams, and money theft. These illegal activities negatively affect society, businesses, and people. Imagine you cannot pass a driving test, even though you know how to drive unless you pay a bribe! Therefore,

Financial crimes will erode victims' confidence in their financial systems and harm the economy.

The Birth

Financial crimes have been present throughout history, including times. While the exact origins are uncertain, individuals discovered ways to exploit systems for their gain as societies became more complex. Throughout history, instances of fraud, corruption, and the production of goods have been documented. The following is a tale.

The Modern Financial Crimes

Financial crimes have become more complicated today, where technology and foreign links are everywhere. It means that criminals have become more capable of breaking the law and worsening the economy; Ponzi scams and financial fraud are all examples of their crimes.

Because financial systems are getting more complicated and people can join and trade worldwide, these scams are happening more often. To protect ourselves and the business, we need to know about these crimes and what happens when they happen. Governments, groups, and people work together to stop and punish financial crimes. This keeps the financial system fair and safe for everyone. lets discuss the most modern financial crimes nowadays:

CORRUPTION

Corruption occurs when people in power abuse their authority for gain, such as benefits, social privileges, or political influence. This problem can take forms like bribery, embezzlement, fraud, or favoritism. Accepting behaviours in our society undermine our institutions' core principles of fairness, impartiality, and trust.

It is undoubtedly the most terrifying crime; its insidious presence can trigger a chain reaction, activating various other criminal activities. It is like a poisonous root that spreads its tendrils throughout society, affecting everything from small businesses to government institutions.

It steals resources and erodes trust and integrity, paving the way for other crimes to flourish. The consequences of corruption are immeasurable. It obstructs progress by diverting resources meant for development towards purposes through the actions of unscrupulous individuals.

Power imbalances create inequality as those with authority exploit the system for their advantage, further disadvantaging others. If individuals perceive corruption within their government and justice system, it can lead to losing trust and confidence in these institutions. Corruption erodes trust in establishments.

Corruption is widespread in regions across the globe which has detrimental effects on the daily lives of local populations. According to Transparency International, an organization dedicated to fighting corruption, more than 50% of countries worldwide are affected by this pervasive issue.

There are different types of corruption which negatively affect society. These include bribery, favoritism, blackmail, illicit payments, extraordinary interest influence, close relationships benefiting from power local bias granting favors, in exchange, for support, misuse of funds and theft. Now, let us define several types on corruption:

Nepotism

Nepotism refers to giving treatment, in employment opportunities, to relatives or close friends without considering their qualifications or merits. This can result in individuals with qualifications being appointed to positions of authority or influence while deserving candidates are overlooked. Such favoritism within networks, among family and friends, undermines trust in established institutions and restricts fair access to opportunities.

Extortion

This refers to the act of obtaining something, either an object or money, by using force, fear, or intimidation. It is a situation where someone, in a position of authority or influence, pressures others to give up their possessions while in a state. For instance, imagine a group pressuring businesses to pay for protection or a government official demanding bribes from individuals in exchange for essential services. Extortion presents a danger to both individuals' well-being and the stability of businesses.

Lobbying

Lobbying is where individuals or groups exert influence over government decisions to further their interests. People use this approach to express their views, concerns and aspirations to lawmakers and policymakers. While lobbying can be a way of voicing perspectives it is crucial to examine its potential impact on the democratic process.

It plays a role in shaping policy and the development of legislation. Lobbying involves organizations and individuals effectively conveying their viewpoints and advocating for their interests. This can include engaging in discussions with lawmakers actively participating in hearings and providing research and specialized knowledge on specific issues.

However, the influence of lobbying can raise concerns about fairness and transparency. Ensuring conduct in lobbying activities is essential to prevent favoritism towards specific groups or interests at the expense of the broader public welfare. Implementing measures that promote transparency and disclosure regarding lobbying activities can effectively uphold accountability.

Cronyism

Cronyism is a phenomenon characterised by preferential

treatment towards individuals who share personal relationships, such as friends, relatives, or close associates. This practice is particularly evident in the allocation of positions or opportunities. This action gives rise to apprehensions regarding the principles of equity, merit-based systems, and the credibility of decision-making mechanisms.

The practice undermines the fundamental principles of equal opportunity and fairness, granting preferential treatment to individuals based on personal connections rather than their merit or qualifications. Therefore, an inefficiency may arise due to the potential reliance on personal connections rather than competence when making decisions regarding appointments and promotions. The detrimental consequences of cronyism can be observed in the public and private sectors. The presence of certain factors can impede the progress of innovation and discourage the cultivation of healthy. Competition undermines the confidence individuals have in institutions.

Moreover, cronyism has the potential to foster a culture characterised by a sense of entitlement, which can, in turn, dissuade highly skilled individuals from actively seeking out and pursuing various opportunities. This is primarily attributed to the prevailing perception that the system is inherently biased and unfair.

To address the issue of cronyism, it is imperative to prioritise the promotion of transparency, accountability, and selection processes based on merit. Establishing a fair and equitable environment in which individuals are assessed based on their abilities, credentials, and accomplishments can alleviate the adverse consequences of cronyism.

Parochialism

This is a phenomenon characterised by the inclination of individuals or collectives to prioritise their limited interests, often to the detriment of broader societal or organizational objectives. Accordingly, biased decisions, restricted collaboration, and impeded progress and development of communities may ensue as a result.

It can be observed in diverse forms, including but not limited to regional favoritism, tribalism, and groupthink. When decision-makers prioritise the interests of a particular group or region, there is a potential for them to disregard the needs and Perspectives of other groups lead to uneven allocation of resources and opportunities. This mindset can obstruct social cohesion, hinder cooperation, and perpetuate societal divisions.

The presence of barriers can impede the effectiveness of problem-solving and compromise, constraining the capacity for collective progress. To surmount parochialism, adopting an inclusive approach that encompasses diversity, encourages participatory decision-making, and facilitates constructive dialogue among diverse stakeholders is imperative.

Patronage

Patronage entails the act of bestowing favors or privileges upon individuals in return for their loyalty, support, or personal benefit. This phenomenon frequently manifests within political and bureaucratic spheres, wherein individuals occupy positions of authority leverage their power to bestow favors upon their loyal followers which could erode the principles of meritocracy, fairness, and accountability.

You would probably agree with me if I said that individuals who obtain jobs or promotions based on their personal connections rather than their qualifications and skills can necessitate the employment of more qualified individuals to back them up. (In other words, it is money down the drain).

Patronage, no doubt, impedes operational effectiveness and undermines the general public's confidence in various establishments. Moreover, it sustains a structure of reliance and fosters a societal mindset characterised by a sense of entitlement.

I can say that it can proliferate and hinder upward social mobility, as individuals lacking influential connections may encounter difficulties accessing opportunities and resources. To avoid this evil act, it is imperative to establish transparent and meritocratic mechanisms for recruitment, promotion, and resource allocation.

Influence peddling

This act refers to using connections, influence, or professional status to gain advantages or special treatment. It involves manipulating decision making processes through means, like bribery, favoritism, and coercion.

Such behaviour has an impact on the principles of fairness, transparency, and the integrity of institutions. It can have reaching consequences by undermining the honesty of services and eroding trust in governance systems. It allows individuals with authority or influential networks to exploit policies, regulations, and contracts for their benefit at the expense of the public's well-being. Have you ever been a witness to an event in which you noticed a celebrity receiving special treatment that was not in accordance with policy?

In reality, it creates an environment of corruption where resources and opportunities are allocated based on connections than merit or qualifications; it leads to hindering competition in the business sector and perpetuates socioeconomic inequalities.

To tackle this issue of influence peddling effectively it is crucial to establish guidelines rigorously enforce measures against corruption and promote transparency in decision making processes. Creating a culture characterized by integrity and accountability is essential in addressing the consequences of influence peddling and ensuring conditions for all stakeholders involved.

Embezzlement

Embezzlement is a form of behaviour where someone unlawfully takes control of entrusted resources, for their own benefit. It commonly occurs within organizations or corporations. This unauthorized appropriation of funds by individuals in positions of authority, such as employees or managers, can have consequences for both the entities involved and the individuals affected.

When someone responsible for management or asset handling misuses funds through embezzlement it negatively impacts the organization's stability and reputation. The repercussions may include losses, bankruptcy, and a loss of trust, from stakeholders.

Those who engage in embezzlement often employ strategies to conceal their illicit activities making detection difficult. They may manipulate records, create documentation or exploit loopholes in internal control systems.

Embezzlement can occur across industries and sectors including entities, nonprofit organizations, government bodies and financial institutions. It's clear that corruption adversely affects our economy in many ways. Although I'm going to cover this topic later, it's helpful at this stage to mention a couple of heavy impacts corruption would create. First, it slows down the growth and development of the economy. Foreign and domestic investments are less likely to happen when corruption is common.

Because there are risks and unknowns in a corrupt environment, investors may hesitate to do business there. This lack of investment slows down new ideas, the creation of jobs, and economic growth. Second, corruption makes the playing field less even. It creates competition unfair by letting dishonest people or businesses get an unfair advantage through bribery, nepotism, or other illegal means. This makes it harder for Honest businesses grow and make it harder to move up in the economy. In the long run, a country with a corrupt economy becomes less competitive globally. This makes it harder for the government to get investments and trade with other countries.

Also, corruption takes money and resources away from critical areas like education, health care, and building infrastructure. Instead of being used for what they were meant to, these resources end up in the hands of corrupt people or are wasted because of inefficient practices. This lack of investment in essential areas hurts social welfare and slows down the growth of our society.

It can have long-term effects that can be hard to fix. Giving everyone the same chances and moving up the social ladder in a corrupt economy can be challenging.

And It makes income inequality worse because people with power and connections are more likely to get money from corrupt practices, while communities that are already struggling are left behind. This kind of inequality can lead to social unrest, political instability, and a lack of trust in institutions, all of which are bad for the economy in the long run.

Grafting

Grafting is the utilization of an individual's position of power or authority for personal benefit through accepting illicit payments, bribes, or kickbacks.

In its various manifestations, corruption poses a significant threat to the fundamental principles of fairness, equality, and accountability within the public and private domains.

It presents a substantial peril to the welfare of societies as it redirects public resources intended for the collective benefit towards the personal gain of individuals engaged in corrupt practices.

Grafting undermines the general public's confidence in various institutions and poses obstacles to economic progress by manipulating fair competition and hindering investment opportunities. It manifests in diverse manners, encompassing bribery, embezzlement, and fraudulent conduct. These illicit activities involve public officials leveraging their positions to solicit or accept bribes for favorable treatment, contracts, or other benefits.

To effectively address graft, it is imperative to establish comprehensive anti-corruption legislation, implement independent oversight mechanisms, and foster a societal ethos prioritizing integrity and accountability. Enhancing transparency, enacting robust safeguards for whistleblowers, and promoting citizen engagement are crucial in uncovering and remedying instances of corruption. Here are some forms of grafting:

Kickbacks

Kickbacks are when someone receives a share of a business deal or contract, as a reward, for giving treatment or influencing decision making. An example of this practice can be seen in contract acquisition, where a supplier offers a kickback to a purchasing manager.

This kind of behaviour distorts competition, drives up prices and undermines the trustworthiness of the decision-making process.

Bribery

Bribery is when someone gives or receives money, gifts, or favors in order to get treatment or gain advantages. It happens when someone offers or accepts a bribe. For instance, one situation could be a student giving money to a teacher in exchange, for a grade. Another scenario might involve a business professional paying a government official to secure a profitable contract. Both of these situations show examples of corruption. Accepting bribes undermines the core principles of fairness and equality by creating an unequal environment.

FRAUD

Fraud refers to deceitful actions carried out with the intention of deceiving others and gaining an advantage. It encompasses a range of practices, such as fraud, identity theft, insurance scams and internet-based schemes. The core components of fraud involve deception, personal or financial gain and the harm caused to individuals who are misled by these activities.

These deceptive practices are aimed at obtaining an advantage or unlawfully acquiring something. They include acts like stealing identities committing credit card fraud, perpetrating scams engaging in investment fraud participating in *Ponzi schemes* orchestrating healthcare frauds executing mortgage scams, performing employment deceptions and defrauding charities. These fraudulent activities involve manipulation, misrepresentation and targeting individuals or organizations for benefit.

Shades Of Fraud

Recognizing the forms of fraud is crucial for protecting oneself against scams and fraudulent schemes. Here are some:

Identity Theft

Identity theft is when someone unlawfully uses another person's information, like their name, Social Security number or financial details with the intention to deceive and defraud that individual.

The victim can face both emotional consequences due to the use of their identity by criminals engaging in fraudulent activities such as creating bank accounts applying for loans or making unauthorized purchases.

Credit Cards

Credit card fraud occurs when an individual utilizes someone's Credit card or credit card details without their consent. This form of fraud involves purchasing cash advances or transferring funds from the victim's account. Fraudsters usually acquire credit cards information through tactics such as phishing, skimming and data breaches. It's one of the most common frauds globally.

Scams Conducted Online

Online scams encompass a range of activities carried out through the internet. These scams include auction fraud, where individuals are deceived into purchasing non-existent or misrepresented products. Phishing scams are also prevalent, with con artists posing as entities to obtain information from unsuspecting victims. Additionally romance scams, work from home scams and lottery scams are forms of deception.

Investment Fraud

Investment fraud involves deceptive practices that promise high returns on investments in fraudulent schemes. Examples of methods include Ponzi schemes, where early investors are paid with funds from investors and pump and dump ways where fraudsters manipulate stock prices for personal gain.

Unfortunately, many investors fail to consider the risks involved and end up suffering losses due to investment fraud. In the insurance context "insurance fraud" refers to the act of making inflated claims to insurance companies for gain. This can involve fabricating accidents to collect insurance benefits, inflating bills, for reimbursement or inventing damage claims related to one's property.

Pump & Dump

Pump and dump is like a sneaky trick played on people in the stock market. Imagine someone telling all their friends that a certain toy is the coolest thing ever, and everyone starts buying it. The price goes up because everyone wants one.

Now, the person who started the rumor sells his toys for a high price.

Then suddenly, everyone realizes the toy isn't that cool after all, and the price crashes. The people who bought the toy late lose money, and the one who started the rumor makes a profit. In the stock market, this trick is illegal, and it's a way that people cheat others to make money. It's like telling a lie to make your friends spend their allowance and then taking advantage of them. Not cool at all!

Insurance Fraud

In the world of insurance "insurance fraud" refers to the act of making exaggerated claims to insurance companies to reap benefits. This can involve fabricating accidents to secure insurance payouts, inflating expenses, or concocting damage claims, for property. Insurance fraud does not lead to losses for insurance providers only, but also results in higher premiums for all policyholders.

Ponzi Schemes

These schemes entail investment operations where the returns promised to investors are funded using money contributed by investors rather than legitimate profits. Ponzi schemes fall into the category of pyramid schemes, which rely on an influx of investors to maintain the facade of profitability. However once new investors dry up the scheme collapses, causing harm to many initial investors.

Healthcare Fraud

Healthcare fraud refers to fraudulent practices within the healthcare industry. Examples include billing for services that were never performed, providing procedures, and engaging in scams related to prescription drugs. Fraud in healthcare can result in increased costs, compromised quality of care for patients and higher insurance premiums.

Mortgage fraud

This occurs when individuals or professionals involved in the mortgage process deceive lenders, borrowers, or property buyers to make a financial gain. Mortgage fraud can be costly for all parties involved. Inflating the value of a property, providing false information about one's income or employment, or submitting fraudulent documents during the mortgage application process are all examples of this practice.

Employment fraud

This type of fraud involves tactics related to job opportunities. It can include job listings scams targeting job applicants or even pyramid schemes that masquerade as employment prospects. Scammers exploit individuals seeking work by soliciting details demanding payments or making unrealistic promises of employment.

Charity Fraud

Charity fraud refers to using dishonest or unethical business practices in connection with charitable organisations or fundraising activities. This can include the misappropriation of donations, deceptive tactics to pursue financial support or the creation of fake charities for personal gain. It destroys the public's trust in charitable organisations and syphons resources away from worthy philanthropic causes.

FRAUD IS AN AWFUL CRIME

In today's world, it is essential for everyone to equip themselves with knowledge regarding the forms of fraud to protect themselves from falling into its traps.

The consequences of fraud extend beyond individuals; it affects both nations and individuals. And on some level, it can result in material losses, identity theft and emotional distress; for example, recovering stolen funds after becoming a victim of information theft can be a battle leaving victims feeling vulnerable and anxious.

The financial burden and emotional toll that follows can cast a shadow on one's well-being. Furthermore, the repercussions of fraud go beyond boundaries, it might affect people's trust in financial systems, institutions, and businesses. Accordingly, the faith in the markets becomes uncertain which hinders growth. And when fraudulent activities go unchecked unethical practices thrive, which dampens the prospects of businesses and investments.

In parallel, society as a bear the weight of the aftermath caused by fraud as individuals and businesses strained by difficulties turn to government resources and services for support. It does not stop there! This strain also extends to taxpayers who may face increased taxes or reduced government assistance for programs.

The impact also contributes to inequality as it targets those who're already disadvantaged while hindering efforts towards achieving economic fairness. To minimize the devastating effects of fraud it is crucial to promote awareness about it while reinforcing regulations and advocating for education.

Having knowledge about scams is crucial as it enables individuals to make choices. Additionally, the collaboration between law enforcement agencies and financial institutions plays a role in strengthening the battle against activities. Believe me, while fraud may appear tempting for achievements it is a trap that ensnares unsuspecting individuals. Later in the book, we'll dive into how financial crimes like these affect us in different ways. It's a big deal, and we'll explore why it matters so much.

DON'T EVEN THINK ABOUT IT!

"Your actions create ripples that extend beyond your own life."

Who doesn't like the idea of easy money? I wish I could tell you the secrets to getting it effortlessly. But here's a sad truth: such a thing doesn't really exist. Don't be fooled by flashy videos promising ways to earn money fast; most of those folks are just trying to get views to make money themselves! Money is valuable and should be earned honestly. The only ways to get 'easy money' are through inheritance, winning lotteries, or engaging in unlawful and unethical activities. And trust me, that last path? It's not worth it.

Engaging in fraud practices does not only damage your future prospects but also undermines your moral compass, shattering trust and leaving a lasting impact on your reputation. The consequences include devastating impacts, shattered dreams, and lifelong regret.

It can be tempting to fall for the appeal of taking shortcuts and seeking gains, especially in a world where the promise of instant success can cloud our judgment. However, let me share with you a more rewarding path—one that guarantees not only your own success but also the happiness and well-being of those around you.

Just take a moment to imagine being responsible for someone's sadness and suffering. Picture yourself as the cause behind their nights, the tears they shed and the dreams they had to let go of. It's a weight to carry one that can leave a lasting impact on your conscience.

While fraudulent activities may offer wealth they ultimately lead to broken trust, shattered relationships, and heartbreak. Every individual bears a responsibility towards those they care about well as even those they don't personally know. You possess the power to bring happiness, inspire others and initiate change. You can choose to uplift someone's spirits, make a difference in their life, and become the reason behind their smile.

As you navigate through this journey think about the legacy you want to leave behind. Choose kindness over dishonesty, empathy over manipulation and truthfulness, over deceit. Your actions have the power to shape your destiny influence others and create a world filled with happiness, trust, and genuine joy. Let your conscience guide you and let your choices reflect the goodness that resides within you. Be the reason someone smiles than cries.

The road to success isn't always the easiest one but it's definitely the most fulfilling. It's about working hard, putting in the effort and achieving your goals with integrity and honesty. And remember, every action you take leaves a mark on your character; *These marks will shape who you are and how you'll be remembered.* True success lies in upholding integrity, working hard and being honest. By choosing the path of integrity you can achieve success, earn respect from others, and build a future based on trust and honor

TERRORIST FINANCING

Terrorism is a term that brings about fear and uncertainty. It encompasses acts of violence, or the threat of violence carried out by individuals or groups with beliefs. These acts aim to instil fear, create chaos and further political or ideological agendas. However, what's even more concerning is how terrorists exploit the system to finance their activities.

The process known as financing involves acquiring, transferring, and utilizing funds or assets to support terrorist acts. It includes money transfers fundraising through various channels and using legal or illegal businesses to generate funds.

It's not weird to think that crimes and terrorist actions could affect young people, but the scary truth is that these bad guys can sometimes trick and influence anyone, even adults! They often target individuals like teenagers who long for belongingness, purpose, or recognition. Through tactics they manipulate young minds and indoctrinate them with extremist ideologies. By targeting teenagers in this way terrorists aim to establish a network of influenced supporters who may eventually provide financial backing for their actions.

The consequences of Terrorist financing are extensive. Economies can become destabilized as funds flow into the hands of terrorists undermining business confidence and hindering growth. And societies , similarly, may suffer as fear and division erode community trust and cohesion. The impact of terrorism on our lives cannot be ignored, as it leads to the loss of innocent lives, the destruction of families and leaves individuals traumatized. It is crucial for teenagers to understand their role in combating financing.

By educating themselves about the tactics employed by terrorists identifying signs of radicalization and reporting activities they can become catalysts for change. Raising awareness is essential in preventing the spread of ideologies and disrupting the financial networks that support terrorism. All young people must come together to oppose terrorism and its financial backing. We need to reject attempts by extremists to manipulate and brainwash us while remaining vigilant in safeguarding our peers from becoming victims of their schemes.

MONEY LAUNDERING IN A NUTSHELL

It is a tactic employed by criminals to hide the origins of obtained money, making it seem like legitimate funds. It's a tool for individuals involved in drug trafficking, corruption, fraud, and organized crime. By channeling their ill profits through intricate financial transactions criminals aim to distance themselves from the illegal activities connected to their bad money. This act in itself is an offense and plays a vital role for wrongdoers in preserving the financial gains acquired through unlawful means. It allows them to enjoy their wealth while minimizing the risk of being detected and prosecuted.

Through disguising the proceeds of their crime, criminals can utilize laundered funds for expenses, investments and expanding their criminal enterprises. This practice undermines the principles of law and erodes trust in financial institutions. Enabled by money laundering techniques, criminals can finance illicit activities leading to higher crime rates and increased violence, within communities. The illicit flow of funds also perpetuates corruption. Weakens the integrity of both governmental and private sector entities. Ultimately money laundering poses a threat to societal stability and security while hindering progress and justice. later In this book we will delve deeper into the topic of money laundering on.

THE CASH COWS IN A NUTSHELL

In this discussion we aim to shed light on criminal activities that deeply concern us such as the trafficking of narcotics and humans, piracy, cybercrime, counterfeiting and corruption. Although these types of crimes may not seem directly relevant to our lives as teenagers, they have a significant impact on the well-being of our communities and our future prospects. Let's delve into the side of these illicit activities and uncover alarming statistics that emphasize the urgent need to combat them.

Narcotics Trafficking

Criminal organizations continue to profit from narcotics trafficking due to the high demand for illegal drugs. These organizations employ networks to smuggle and distribute drugs across borders while evading law enforcement. The money generated from narcotics trafficking doesn't just benefit criminals; it perpetuates crime and addiction creating a dangerous cycle that harms individuals and communities. It's an issue that demands our attention.

According to the United Nations Office, on Drugs and Crime (UNODC) the global illegal drug market is valued at hundreds of billions of dollars. This staggering amount highlights the gravity of this problem. We cannot ignore this issue; we must take action and make a positive impact. For instance, in the United States, drug abuse has had an economic toll, with the cost estimated to be over $740 billion in 2019. This includes expenses related to healthcare lost productivity, and the criminal justice system (National Institute on Drug Abuse, NIDA). According to statistics from the United Nations, illicit drugs generate an estimated revenue of $400 billion.

Human Trafficking

It is a crime that preys on vulnerable individuals who are desperate for financial stability. It involves buying, selling, and forcing people into labor or sexual exploitation. Traffickers often manipulate their victims through deceit, coercion, or physical violence. The immense profits derived from this heartless trade perpetuate a cycle of exploitation. Therefore, it is crucial to raise awareness and support initiatives aimed at rescuing victims and prosecuting those criminals.

According to the International Labor Organization (ILO) around 25 million people worldwide fall victim to trafficking every year. This includes forced labor and sexual exploitation. It is estimated that criminal organizations make $150 billion in profits annually from human trafficking (United Nations Office on Drugs and Crime UNODC).

Piracy

With the advent of the age comes new forms of piracy where criminals unlawfully reproduce and distribute copyrighted materials.

The problem of piracy poses a challenge for content creators and the creative industries, causing them substantial financial losses. Not only does piracy harm artists financially, but it also hampers innovation and creativity by discouraging the production of new and diverse content. The scale of piracy remains a pressing issue. According to Digital TV Research, the global value of piracy in movies, TV shows, music and software was estimated to be approximately $29.4 billion in 2020.

In 2019 the film industry suffered an estimated loss of $6.8 billion due to online piracy (Motion Picture Association). These figures have seen an increase between 2022, with estimates ranging from $29 billion to $71 billion annually.

Cybercrimes

In terms of cybercrime, criminals are constantly adapting their tactics to target individuals, businesses, and financial institutions. They employ techniques like phishing, ransomware attacks, and identity theft to gain unauthorized access to sensitive data and financial assets.

Apprehending these criminals proves challenging due to the internet's anonymity and global reach. This highlights the need for robust cybersecurity measures and public awareness campaigns aimed at protecting against cyber threats.

The economic impact of cybercrime is staggering; projections indicate that global losses will surpass $6 trillion annually by 2021 (Cybersecurity Ventures). In the United States, data breaches cost an average of $3.86 million in 2020, according to IBM Security. Even small businesses are at risk, with 43% of cyberattacks targeting them as stated in Verizon's 2021 Data Breach Investigations Report. Statista's Cybersecurity Outlook predicts that the global cost of cybercrime will increase from $8.44 trillion in 2022 to $13.84 trillion in 2028 over five years.

Counterfeiting

It is an issue worldwide where dishonest traders flood markets with fake products that mimic reputable brands. These counterfeit goods exploit the popularity of known brands to deceive unsuspecting buyers. Apart from eroding consumer trust, counterfeit items can also pose health and safety hazards, especially in pharmaceuticals and electronics. It is crucial to raise awareness about the prevalence and risks associated with products to safeguard consumers and support legitimate businesses.

Counterfeit goods make up 3.3% of global trade, resulting in nearly $500 billion in annual losses according to the International Chamber of Commerce (ICC). And the European Union Intellectual Property Office (EUIPO) estimates that counterfeit products accounted for 6.8% of imports into the EU in 2019 leading to significant economic damages. Also, According to a report by the OECD the global market for pirated goods was valued at approximately $1 trillion in 2013 and it is projected to reach nearly $3 trillion by 2022.

Corruption

I know that we have covered this crime earlier, but it's worth mentioning again. We fave This issue infiltrates different sectors of society including public officials and private businesses. When individuals entrusted with power misuse their positions for gain, it leads to allocating public funds and resources. Corruption does not impede economic growth but also contributes to inequality and erodes public trust in institutions.

Addressing corruption requires ethical leadership, transparent governance and an engaged citizenry that holds wrongdoers accountable. Its impact on economies and societies worldwide is significant. It is estimated that corruption costs 5% of global GDP annually amounting to roughly $2.6 trillion according to the United Nations Development Program (UNDP). Also, the Transparency Internationals Corruption Perceptions Index 2020 reveals that two thirds of countries scored below 50 (out of 100) on the index indicating corruption in many parts of the world.

As we delve into profitable illicit activities it becomes crucial to grasp their extensive consequences. These financial crimes are not about monetary aspects; they cause harm to individuals, communities, and societies, as a whole. According to the Corruption Statistics provided by "Transparency International UK " it is estimated that the global cost of corruption including bribes and embezzled funds reaches $3.6 trillion annually.

THE WORLD OF DARK SPIRITS

In this discussion we will explore the realms of big-time

players and shadowy worlds encompassing a diverse range of individuals involved in these spheres. The characters that populate these domains vary greatly from professionals to seasoned criminals.

By understanding the functions and behaviors of these individuals we can paint a more accurate picture of how financial crimes manifest in the real world.

My aim here is to offer you insights into the intricacies of different types of financial criminals. By familiarizing yourself with the players and attempting to comprehend their motivations, you will better understand the underlying factors that drive these illicit activities.

As a teenager you may have some experience and confidence in dealing with the challenges of your world. However, when it comes to dealing with the 'Dark World' things become more complex.

Thinking you can handle this world just because you have some experience is like getting too confident too fast. It's just not right. In this place, there are sneaky people who will do anything to prey on their victims and trick others into joining them. They twist the truth to make their actions seem okay, and they know how to get to people. They might even target teenagers, using their feelings and weaknesses against them.

They appeal to desires for strength, desirability, value, success, respect, or wealth. They might convince you that "Robin Hood" is more than a fictional character and make you believe that his actions represent true justice. Essentially making it seem like doing the wrong thing is actually correct. It is crucial to differentiate between teachings and any malevolent ideas disguised as ethical intentions that could result in criminal thinking and a lack of empathy. Never *fall for such brainwashing schemes.*

In a world where things are not always as they seem, teenagers must grasp the true character of individuals engaged in financial crimes. The following discussion aims to provide insight into individuals involved in illicit financial schemes. It emphasises the significance of assessing people based on the patterns of their actions, behaviour, and mindsets rather than solely relying on their external appearance. Teenagers must exercise caution and discernment when deciding whom to trust, whether white-collar criminals, influential figures, diplomats, or even those in government positions. As the saying goes, "The image captured by a camera lens may only depict a fraction, perhaps less than 10%, of the true reality."

To protect yourself from potential exploitation or deception, as a teenager, you should develop the skill of validating and evaluating any factors that promote a change before fully embracing it; talk to your parents, teachers, and long-time trusted elders; don't rely on your views only. I'm not underestimating your capabilities; I suggest considering extra views.

The White Collar

You may have encountered the term "white collar offenses" before. These are crimes committed by individuals, in attire and formal environments. Despite appearing professional and reliable there is often business happening behind doors. As people it's essential for us to be vigilant about these offenses, which encompass deceit, fraud, and the illicit use of money.

The Deceptive Influencers

Now, let's talk about those social media influencers we see everywhere. They share inspiring ideas and positive messages, which is incredible. But guess what! Some of them might not be as genuine as they appear.

Some influencers might promote stuff connected to shady ways of making money. They make it look so appealing, like we could have it all, but we need to be cautious and not believe everything they say. It's crucial to question and think about whether their claims are valid. In these circles, Corruption is the most common crime than we'd like to think, even in diplomatic and government circles which we will touch base shortly. It isn't enjoyable, I know. These people should be looking out for us and our countries, but some use their positions to benefit themselves.

They might engage in bribery, theft, or money laundering, all for their own gain. But hold on; not everyone in power acts that way. We should focus on their actions, their integrity, and how much they genuinely care about doing what's suitable for everyone.

So, you can't always trust what you see. When it comes to people involved in financial crimes, it's crucial to see beyond the surface. Our discussion sheds light on the individuals caught up in these illegal schemes. It reminds us to pay attention to how people act and what they stand for, not just their outward appearances. We need to be thoughtful and careful about whom we trust and follow, whether it's slick white-collar criminals, powerful figures, or government officials.

Always keep in mind that a picture you see and like may only capture a small part of someone's life. So Before we wholeheartedly trust someone, we need to find out more and decide if they deserve our trust. By doing this, we'll make informed decisions and safeguard our future from unexpected risks. So, remember that white-collar crimes aren't always obvious. People who appear to be respectable on the outside but are dishonest inside commit these crimes. Understanding this reality will help us avoid falling for their manipulative tactics and protect ourselves from getting tangled up in deceitful webs. I'm not advising you to be overly skeptical or to question everyone's integrity. I'm just recommending that you refrain from giving anyone a big portion of trust unless you've really done your due diligence.

The Diplomat And Government Official Relations

As said, corruption and financial crimes can also infiltrate the realm of diplomacy and governments. While diplomats and government officials have the duty of serving their countries and advancing the welfare of their citizens there are instances where some individuals exploit their positions, for personal gain.

They may resort to bribery, embezzlement or money laundering leveraging their power and authority for benefits. Young people need to understand that not everyone in a position upholds moral standards and it is important to assess individuals based on their actions, integrity, and dedication to the greater good.

Nevertheless, it is vital to approach accusations of corruption or criminal activities with caution. We should not hastily label a government official as corrupt based on assumptions. Instead, our responsibility lies in reporting any occurrences or activities to the authorities.

By taking actions we actively contribute to uncovering the truth and ensuring investigations are conducted. We must handle these matters diligently while adhering to procedures in addressing any concerns we may have. here are few steps you can follow when encounter or notice a corrupted "GO":

- Don't Confront the Individual Directly: It might be tempting to confront the person, but this could be risky, especially if the person involved holds a position of power.

- Talk to a Trusted Adult: If you notice something that doesn't seem right, talk to a parent, teacher, or another adult you trust. They can help you figure out the best course of action.

- Gather Information: If it's safe to do so, take note of what you saw or heard. Details can be important.

- Stay Safe: Your safety is the most important thing. If you ever feel in danger tell someone you trust.

- Report if Necessary: Depending on the situation, the trusted adult might advise you to report what you've seen to the authorities or another appropriate entity.

- Learn from the Experience: Understanding the importance of ethics, honesty, and integrity is a valuable lesson. Discuss with mentors or educators about these values to grow your understanding of what's right.

The Preachers Of Deception

Even those who claim to be religious or spiritual leaders can sometimes manipulate their followers for personal gain. While it is essential to respect religious freedom and diversity, teenagers must be cautious when evaluating the teachings and actions of preachers.

Some individuals may exploit their religious authority to persuade others to contribute financially to illegal activities. Teenagers should seek wisdom and guidance from trusted sources, critically examining the teachings and actions of preachers to ensure they align with the values of compassion, respect, and ethical conduct.

The Blue Collar

Blue-collar crime refers to criminal activities committed by individuals from working-class or manual labor backgrounds. These crimes typically involve more direct and visible forms of criminal behaviour, often associated with violence or property offenses.

This type of crime is generally less sophisticated and more easily detectable than white-collar crimes, which involve more complex and non-violent offenses committed by individuals in professional or business settings. Some common examples of blue-collar crimes include theft, burglary, assault, vandalism, and drug-related offenses.

Those criminals can certainly engage in financial crimes, but it's essential to understand that the term "blue-collar crime" typically refers to a specific set of offenses that are more directly related to physical actions or property offenses.

On the other hand, financial crimes, such as fraud, embezzlement, money laundering, and other white-collar crimes, are usually associated with individuals in professional or business settings. These crimes are more complex and often involve manipulation, deception, and misuse of financial resources. While there can be an overlap between different types of criminals and criminal activities, the terms "blue-collar crime" and "financial crime" are generally used to describe different categories of offenses.

There can be interactions between white-collar criminals and blue-collar criminals, especially in the context of certain criminal activities or organized crime networks. While they may come from different backgrounds and engage in different types of offenses, criminals from both groups may collaborate and intersect in certain situations.

For example:

-   In Money Laundering: Blue-collar criminals involved in activities such as drug trafficking, illegal gambling, or robbery may seek to launder their illicit proceeds. They might turn to white-collar criminals, such as financial professionals or accountants, who have the expertise to help them conceal the origins of their money and integrate it into the legitimate financial system.

- Bribery and Corruption: Blue-collar criminals seeking to avoid legal consequences for their actions might attempt to bribe law enforcement officials or other authorities. White-collar criminals with connections in government or positions of power could facilitate such bribery schemes.

- Organized Crime: Both blue-collar and white-collar criminals can be involved in organized crime syndicates. They might collaborate in activities like human trafficking, drug distribution, or extortion, leveraging each other's skills and resources to achieve their criminal objectives. It's important to note that while interactions can occur, many white-collar criminals and blue-collar criminals tend to operate in their respective domains. Each group has its own methods, motivations, and areas of expertise. However, in certain criminal networks or situations, they may find common ground and cooperate to further their criminal activities.

THE MOTIVATION

In our exploration of "Uncovering Motivation," we aim to shed light on what drives individuals to commit financial crimes. The human psyche is complex, and money's power to shape our world can sometimes lead to corruption and deceit. What lures some people into such unlawful paths?

The answer might be found in the psychology of money. Understanding its profound impact on our thoughts and actions offers insight into the motivations behind financial crimes. The allure of quick wealth or a desire for power can create a dangerous cocktail, leading individuals down a treacherous path.

But the story doesn't end with personal greed or ambition. Criminals often specifically target teenagers, recognizing their promise and potential yet exploiting their vulnerabilities. By examining why they make this sinister choice, we hope to empower young people with the knowledge and awareness needed to safeguard themselves.

Beyond the immediate allure of financial gains, we must delve deeper into the minds of those who commit these crimes. Twisted beliefs and creeds can shape actions, providing warped justifications for illicit deeds. Unraveling these complex belief systems reveals even more about what motivates these actions.

As we dissect the roots of financial crimes, we're not only looking at a dark corner of human behavior but working towards a more secure future. Understanding these motivations equips us with the tools to protect ourselves and others. Our journey into the intriguing realm of financial crimes is more than an academic exercise; it's a guide towards safety and awareness in a world where money's allure can lead to unthinkable choices.

The Psychology of Money

Money goes beyond being a medium of exchange; it holds symbolic meaning representing power, success, and social status. Simply being around money can evoke feelings of self-determination and influence that shape how we see the world and make choices.

Studies indicate that money's symbolic power fulfills some of our needs like safety, independence, and social recognition. This creates an environment where both legal and illegal activities thrive.

Our consumerist mindset and materialistic psychology greatly influence our consumer culture defining our values related to material possessions, pleasure, and success. As a result, some individuals resort to practices in order to accumulate wealth and improve their social standing while others do not.

The underlying cause for these differences lies in our consumer culture. Psychological research highlights the impact of a sense of entitlement and the human tendency to rationalize our actions; When exposed to an environment where illegal money is involved, people may develop a sense of entitlement leading them to believe they deserve wealth and advantages.

This entitlement can lead individuals to justify behaviour in pursuit of gain, often finding ways to rationalize the harm caused by their illegal actions. Moreover, when happiness, success and satisfaction are taken to levels they can give rise to self-centered mindsets that foster qualities such, as destructive greed, Ugly apathy, and incompetence.

Let me clarify that I'm not disputing the impact of money on achieving success, happiness, or satisfaction. I suggest that an excessive amount of these emotions can lead to a dependency on wealth and a tendency to seek shortcuts while disregarding considerations. In fact, individuals may even create justifications to suppress any feelings of guilt that may arise in the future.

Why Do People Commit Financial Crimes?

People engage in unlawful financial activities for several reasons, such as greed, apathy, or incompetence.

Their lack of self-assurance and incapacity to confront life's challenges may lead them to resort to sheltered lying to satisfy their hunger for easy rewards.

In their view, financial criminals have distinct ways of thinking that set them apart from others. Some people are driven by greed, desiring to get rich quickly at the cost of others may find possibilities to scam the system and get fast money. Others might commit financial crimes because they are desperate or believe they deserve more than they have. These criminals frequently lack empathy, take risks, and act without considering the consequences.

They may mislead others, participate in insider trading, or steal money from individuals or corporations. Their objectives might range from wanting to live in luxury lifestyle to seeking anger or causing financial chaos. They take advantage of loopholes and naive people to exploit gaps in our financial systems. Of course, they can deceive people into giving them money or utilize their positions of authority to enrich themselves while avoiding penalties by manipulating facts.

The Root Cause

"Root cause" and "motivation" are related but frequently interchangeable concepts. The root cause is the fundamental underlying reason or source that leads to a specific problem or issue. The initial event starts a chain of events that results in a specific outcome or behaviour. Understanding the deeper factors contributing to a problem is critical for identifying the root cause, as addressing the root cause can help prevent the issue from recurring. On the other hand, motivation is the inner drive or incentive that drives an individual to act in a certain way or pursue a specific goal. The underlying reason or purpose drives and directs behaviour. Motivation can be intrinsic (driven by personal desires or values) or extrinsic (influenced by external rewards or consequences).

The Impact of Inequality and Social Comparison

Societal and economic inequalities can contribute to the emergence of illicit finance. According to several studies, economically disadvantaged people who experience relative deprivation sentiments are more likely to turn to Illegal measures to make up the difference.

Social comparison or comparing oneself to others in terms of their financial position and belongings, can exacerbate these emotions of disparity and inspire the urge to achieve similar amounts of riches through illicit actions.

The Relationship Between Risk and Reward

The prospect of significant cash gains frequently makes people engage in illegal financial activity. The human brain is hardwired to react to the prospect of future benefits, which causes dopamine release, motivating behaviour that involves taking risks. This brain reaction could override ethical considerations, causing individuals to participate in illegal actions to achieve significant financial gains.

The Shadow Part of Human Psychology

Recent studies on how our minds work have shown a link between certain ways of thinking and illegal activities with money. If someone thinks in a way that's sneaky and dishonest (this is called the Machiavellian worldview), they might use other people to get what they want. Or if someone lacks feelings for others and doesn't really know right from wrong (this is known as psychopathy), they might commit financial crimes without feeling guilty.

Fear and the Search for Security

Money is a big part of how safe and happy we feel. Research

shows that financial insecurity and the fear of Losing money can make people take drastic steps, such as using illegal money, to protect their futures. People afraid of being left behind or having money problems may choose short-term gains over long-term consequences, leading to unethical and illegal behaviour.

The Effects of Jealousy and Comparing People

Envy is a complicated emotion that comes from wanting what other people have. It can make people want to be rich and unhappy with their financial situation. Studies have shown that people who feel envious may be more likely to do illegal things to close the gap they see between themselves and the people they envy.

When people compare themselves to others in terms of their money and possessions, it can make them feel more envious and make them more likely to use illegal means to get what they want.

The Influence of the Environment

While external factors such as socioeconomic disparities, limited opportunities, and a culture of corruption can all contribute to the prevalence of financial crimes, it is critical to recognise that the decision to engage in illicit finance ultimately rests with the individual.

Environmental factors may provide fertile ground for the emergence of financial criminals, but personal choice plays a critical role in the decision-making process.

WHY FINANCIAL CRIMINALS WOULD TARGET TEENAGERS?

We've touched on this topic before, but now we're going to delve deeper into it.

As a teen, it's essential to know why criminals specifically target your age group. They take advantage of the fact that you are weak, trusting, and want to be alone. They want to trick and take advantage of you using your limited money and manipulative techniques.

For instance, the advent of the digital age has given criminals fresh avenues for exploiting social media and online scams to harvest personal information. But let's dive into some of the underlying reasons.

Vulnerability: Criminals see teenagers as easy targets because they don't know much about the darkness of the crime-world or have little experience with it.

They often trust others, and overestimate their ability to know black from white, making them more vulnerable to manipulation and deceit. Criminals take advantage of teenagers' desire for freedom and independence by telling them they can do things independently and have fun.

Teenagers often don't have much money, and even if they're well-off, their parents might control how they spend it. This situation can make them a target for scammers. They might be tempted by promises of quick, easy money and agree to work with scammers, hoping to save up secretly. But the truth is, scammers will try to take all of their money, no matter how much they have.

Also, because teens use the digital world so much, they're more exposed to digital exploitation. This is when criminals take advantage of their online presence, using social media and online scams to steal personal information and engage in other illegal activities.

Peer pressure: Teenagers are often in a stage of life when they feel like it's very important to fit in and be liked by their friends. They want to be liked, respected, and seen as "cool" or brave. This need to be a part of the group can make them do things they wouldn't normally do. here is how peer pressure could affect teens' mindsets:

- Taking risks: Peer pressure can lead teens to do things that are risky or even dangerous, like trying drugs or doing things that are against the law. It could be as simple as a dare or a challenge, or it could be a way to show loyalty to a group.

- Peer pressure online and on social media: In the digital age we live in now, peer pressure doesn't just happen in person. When teens see their friends and even strangers doing exciting or risky things online, it can make them want to do the same. This can make people want to act the same way, even if it's dangerous or against the law.

- Criminals can take advantage of this weakness in teenagers if they know about it. They might pretend to be friends or influential people to get teens to share personal information, send money, or do other bad things. Teens might agree because they want to be liked or accepted, even if they don't fully understand what will happen.

- Effects on Judgement and Making Decisions: Peer pressure can make it hard for teenagers to make good decisions. Even people who usually make good choices might find it hard to say no when they want to be a part of something so much. This makes them less able to think for themselves, which makes them easier to manipulate and can have long-term effects.

Lack of Knowledge: Many teenagers don't know the tricks and methods that criminals use, which makes them more susceptible to manipulation and scams.

Emotional Manipulation: Criminals take advantage of the fact that teenagers are emotionally weak and use techniques like "love bombing" and "fear tactics" to control and take advantage of them.

Individuals who have become corrupt are capable of manipulating and deceiving others via the use of charm and persuasion in order to accomplish their own self-serving aims while ignoring the negative effects of their actions.

CREED: Creed is a term that can be associated with the religious, philosophical, or ideological systems that shape our values and our sense of right and wrong. It's different from religion, which refers to various faith-based practices and communities. Creed is part of our daily lives, guiding our perceptions, actions, and reactions.

Advanced criminals know this, and they understand how to analyze teens' exposure to the ideologies they encounter. They then craft creeds that serve their malicious agendas. In this way, they can manipulate beliefs to steer people in directions that further their own interests.

As a teen, you should be aware of the complex dynamics surrounding ideologies and beliefs and the possibility that these matters can be exploited in today's interconnected world.

The following few points discuss creed, specifically what i call "Twisted and Warped Creeds," and their relationship to the world of financial crimes. My goal is not to stigmatize or generalize any religion or belief system; instead, I want to arm you with the knowledge and understanding to recognise warning signs and protect yourself from the manipulation of warped creeds.

Its quiet unlikely to develop criminal mindsets without a clear reason, purpose, circumstances, motivations or other factors.

Some people are determined to reach their goals, like climbing mountains, and will do whatever it takes. Others might feel trapped by a lack of opportunities, limited resources, or feeling left out by society.

These challenges may lead them to seek alternative paths, even if it means getting involved in criminal activities. Individuals facing these difficulties might justify crime as a way to gain power, wealth, or recognition, or to rebel against what society expects from them.

Twisted and Warped Creeds: The Pawns & The Recruiters

I've never encountered a religion that encourages or adapts to financial crime or financial criminal mindsets. Let me share an essential theory developed through my research and experience in financial criminology. In our lives, we develop two types of knowledge: theoretical and practical.

Theoretical knowledge comes from our studies and research, giving us a foundation of information and ideas. Practical knowledge, on the other hand, is gained from our interaction with the world around us, our experiences and observations.

Whether we like or dislike our surroundings, our theoretical knowledge certainly influences our feelings towards the world. However, it's often our practical knowledge—the wisdom we gain from real-life experiences—that has a more substantial impact on our decisions, actions, and reactions. This hands-on understanding helps us navigate the complexities of life, guiding us in ways that mere theories may not. For example, thieves may understand theoretically that stealing is wrong and condemned by society. But they may still engage in theft due to the ideologies they've adopted from interacting with the wrong influences. Associating with people who twist morals and justify wrongdoing can lead individuals to accept what's usually considered wrong as something right. This illustrates how practical experience and the influences we expose ourselves to can significantly shape our actions, even overriding what we know to be ethically correct.

I like to call this balance the '60-40 setup.' It's a mix of the environment we interact with and our independent thoughts shaped by our knowledge. Even though our surroundings and beliefs have a big influence on us, they don't set our path in stone. They can trigger different reactions, either going along with or challenging what's around us.

We often hear inspiring stories of individuals who were raised in neighborhoods or societies that might promote or tolerate criminality, yet they managed to take a stand against this path. Their reactions to their surroundings were not conformity but defiance. Despite facing challenges and pressures, these people have chosen to pursue legitimate and honorable lives, often driven by the very influences they rejected. Such examples remind us that our reactions to our surroundings are complex and multifaceted. They demonstrate the strength of human character and the ability of individuals to rise above their circumstances, making choices that align with their true selves, whether that means embracing or resisting the influences around them.

In practical terms, the 60-40 setup can be seen as the seed of our wellbeing. Our humanity is the core that needs nurturing with balanced and positive knowledge. The 40% of our mindset gained from knowledge can guide and steer the direction of the 60% gained from our surroundings, helping us decide whether to align with or oppose certain ideologies and paths. while most creeds are rooted in religious, philosophical, or ideological foundations that promote peace, compassion, and harmony, there are instances where specific ideological systems can distort and manipulate creeds, giving rise to twisted and warped versions.

In some cases, extremist ideologies can exploit and twist existing creeds to serve their agenda. These ideologies often propagate a distorted interpretation of religious or ideological teachings, emphasizing violence, intolerance, radicalism, and unethical financial activities. They may selectively highlight certain aspects of a creed while ignoring or distorting its core principles of love, compassion, and respect for human life to create and normalize an ugly apathy.

Such ideologies frequently manipulate creeds to gain power, exercise control, advance a particular political or social agenda or pursue financial gains. These ideologies create an environment by distorting a creed's original teachings and values.

Individuals may be persuaded to engage in acts of violence, terrorism, or other forms of criminal behaviour, such as money laundering, fraud, and terrorist financing, in the name of their distorted beliefs. It is crucial to recognise that these twisted and warped creeds do not represent the true essence of the original creed or the broader community that adheres to it. They result from deliberate manipulation and distortion, often by a minority who seek to exploit vulnerable individuals and propagate their extremist ideologies.

Understanding the distinction between genuine creeds and their twisted counterparts is essential to combating the influence of these warped ideologies. For example, consider a peaceful religious creed that advocates for love, compassion, and unity among its followers.This creed highlights the significance of kindness, forgiveness, and assisting those in need. On the contrary, imagine another radical ideological system emerges in a specific region, motivated by political ambitions and a thirst for power and wealth; In this ideological system, a group of individuals manipulates and distorts the original teachings of the peaceful creed to align with their agenda. They use selective interpretation of specific verses or passages, often taken out of context, to promote ideas of superiority, animosity towards those outside their group, and the endorsement of violence and deception to accomplish their goals.

As these distorted beliefs continue to circulate among susceptible individuals, the fundamental principles of love and compassion that the creed embodies are overshadowed by extremist ideologies.

The created 'Twisted Creed' would rationalise acts of terrorism, discrimination, oppression, and deception against individuals who do not conform to its distorted beliefsIn the criminal underworld, two distinct but interconnected types of creeds can be observed, each playing a unique role in carrying out malicious agendas.

The 'Twisted Creeds' are those who have been indoctrinated into accepting and justifying violent behavior, intolerance, and extreme actions. They are not the masterminds but the foot soldiers, the 'pawns' in a broader scheme. They act without questioning, driven by a misguided sense of righteousness, focusing solely on executing the plans laid out for them. On the other side are those with 'Warped Creeds,' the chess-players in this scenario. These individuals, referred to as 'Recruiters,' are tasked with manipulating and brainwashing others. Unlike the pawns, they don't resort to force or direct intimidation but use more subtle and insidious means to achieve their goals. They adopt long-term strategies, slowly and methodically working to twist the mindsets of those they target.

These 'Recruiters' are incredibly skilled and persuasive. They study their prey, gaining their trust and respect before identifying the perfect moment to plant their toxic ideas. Their approach is akin to a slow-spreading cancer, gradually corrupting the thoughts and beliefs of those they target. The interaction between these two creeds creates a dangerous and powerful dynamic, where warped beliefs lead to twisted actions, all orchestrated by those who see others merely as tools to be used in their grand plans.

Trust me when I tell you that recruiters and pawns can be anywhere; there is a high chance that one day you might interact with one at work, at the club, at the gym, school, or even through familiar friends. Therefore, when interacting with them, teenagers must be able to detect warning signs or red flags, protect themselves, and prevent being exploited or brainwashed; and of course, report them.

The following red flags (aka Warning Sign) may not be exclusive but should help you to identify suspicious behaviour or relationship:

- Criminals might try to trick you by using fear, pressure, or promises of big rewards. They'll ask you to make some changes that might seem really strange at first. Now, making changes isn't always a bad thing, but the changes these bad guys want you to make are different. First, they're not the usual kind of changes; second, most people would say they're just plain wrong; and third, they could hurt you or someone else.

- They might aim to Isolate and shield your world from any external factor promoting opposing views, such as your parents, teachers, or older siblings. They might encourage extremism while discouraging inquiry and independent thoughts. They will concentrate on isolating you from any factor that might interfere with their plans! For example, they may request you to refrain from discussing these ideologies with your parents or older siblings or persuade you to avoid any reference they have not approved of or drifting off their beliefs.

- They may promote or glorify illegal activities under the guise of religious or ideological justifications. They may claim their way is the only way to accomplish intended good deeds, such as funding sanctioned extremists to fight sin, corruption, or whatever else you commonly condemn.

- They might try to convince you to accept the concept of collateral damage where it is acceptable to harm a few to benefit many.

- They may always promote themselves as the only group that correctly practices religion and express their hate to anyone opposing their way.

- They might embrace Intolerance and prejudice, noting that Pawns usually foster hostility, discrimination, and prejudice against others based on their beliefs, ethnicity, or background. These mindsets breed division which can justify harmful actions against innocent people. Although they may not recruit you, pawns may unintentionally expose their dark sides by sharing and hailing violent clips of criminals fighting crime. If you notice any of the scenarios mentioned, it might indicate that you are being recruited or a pawn looming in your area; therefore, you should immediately inform your parents or elders you trust. It is worth noting that if a pawn notices a potential for recruitment, they will escalate the opportunity to their superiors/ recruiters, who will step in.

In general, distinguishing between genuine religious teachings and destructive manipulation of beliefs for evil is critical and challenging. So, remember that ideological systems can significantly impact societies and individuals, shaping their values, beliefs, and behaviours. Therefore, understanding different ideological systems allows you to analyze and engage safely with the big boys' world whenever required. You can protect yourself and your community from the destructive consequences by cultivating a discerning mindset, speaking out against intolerance, and learning to recognise the red flags associated with twisted and warped creeds.

CHAPTER TWO:
THE CONCERN

These days, we all know that teenagers face lots of challenges with money. Some might think that crimes like fraud or identity theft are just adult problems. But that's not true! Financial crimes can affect anyone, even teenagers. So, it's crucial for young people to understand these risks to protect themselves and their future.

In this chapter, we're going to dive into why being aware of financial crimes is so important for teenagers. During your teen years, you start to think about big dreams, independence, and even earning your own money. It's exciting, but it also means you need to be smart about money and aware of the risks.

Financial crimes aren't just one thing. They include fraud (when someone tricks you out of your money), embezzlement (stealing money from a place where you work), money laundering (making illegally gained money look legal), identity theft (someone pretending to be you), and cybercrimes (crimes done online). Criminals doing these things don't just risk your money; they threaten your personal and financial safety. If controls against these crimes are weak, illegal activities can easily grow. Logical reasoning and real-life evidence both say, 'Yes, this is a big deal!' But don't worry, teenagers can make a difference by being aware of these crimes. Sneaky people might try to trick you into illegal activities, but you can be one step ahead by knowing what to look out for.

Financial crimes don't just stop at losing money. If someone steals your identity, it could ruin your credit. This might make it hard for you to get loans for things like college or buying your first car. And being involved in these crimes, even by accident, can harm your reputation and limit your opportunities.

Parents, teachers, and other responsible adults are super important in helping you understand all of this. If anything seems weird or unusual, always talk to someone you trust.

We're going to dig deep into this subject in this chapter. We'll look at real-life examples, explore different risks, and see how these crimes can directly affect teenagers. Our main goal? To help you build strong financial knowledge and resilience so you can confidently navigate the complicated world of money.

THE RISK

Risk is like taking a chance that something might go wrong. It's like trying to figure out what could happen if you make a certain choice or do something specific. Understanding risk is a big deal, especially for teenagers. It helps you make smart choices and steer clear of danger. Think of risk like deciding to jump off a one-story house. Sure, it might be thrilling, but what if you twist an ankle or break a hip? If you have a car driving test the next day, that risk might be too high. But if you're a great jumper, maybe the risk doesn't seem that bad. Now, imagine jumping with a blindfold on – that's way riskier, right?

The important thing is to know the risks you're taking and feel good about them. Don't let things like greed, laziness, or bad judgment lead you into taking chances you're not comfortable with. Sometimes life throws curveballs, and things happen that are out of our control. But by understanding risk, you're setting yourself up to make better decisions and handle whatever comes your way.

The big takeaway is to make sure you understand the risks you're taking and feel okay with them. Don't let greed, laziness, or bad judgment mess up your decisions about how much risk to take.

THE CONSEQUENCES

The following are some potential outcomes of financial crimes, whether you are the victim or the offender; as you read, think about which ones you would be willing to accept:

- Financial Loss and Scams: Teens are vulnerable to various financial scams, resulting in significant financial losses and undermining their trust in others. This can impact their ability to manage their money wisely and save for the future.

- Damaged Credit and Reputation: Even unknowingly, involvement in financial crimes can harm a teen's credit score and reputation. This may make it difficult to obtain financial services or secure loans in the future.

- Emotional Distress: Being a victim of financial crime can result in feelings of betrayal, anger, and anxiety. Such experiences can harm a teenager's mental health and self-esteem.

- Legal Consequences: Financial crimes, even if committed inadvertently, can result in legal consequences for teenagers. This could include fines, probation, or even imprisonment, affecting their prospects and opportunities.

- Loss of Opportunities: Because of their tarnished reputation, teens involved in financial crimes may miss out on valuable opportunities such as educational scholarships, job opportunities, or extracurricular activities.

- Impact on Education: Financial crimes can divert teenagers' attention from their studies and educational goals, harming their academic performance and limiting their long-term career prospects.

- Trust and Peer Relationships: Being deceived or involved in financial crimes can erode trust in friendships and relationships, leading to isolation and difficulty forming new connections in the future.

- Personal Growth Stifled: Being involved in financial crimes can stifle a teenager's personal growth and development.

They may miss valuable life lessons and experiences that will help them mature and make better decisions.

- Long-term Financial Instability: Financial crimes can derail a teen's path to financial stability, making achieving financial independence and a secure future more difficult.

- Recovery Difficulties: Recovering from the effects of financial crimes can take a long time and effort, affecting teenagers' ability to focus on their dreams and goals.

Teenagers may lose trust in financial systems and institutions due to their involvement in financial crimes, making them hesitant to engage in legitimate financial activities.

Financial crimes can strain relationships with parents and family members, resulting in tension and conflict within the home.

And there are several factors can increase the chances of being exposed to or becoming a financial criminal during the teenage years.

THE FACTORS

Risk factors are specific things that can increase the likelihood of a particular negative outcome or danger happening. They're like clues or signs that point to a greater chance of something going wrong.

So, if the risk is being exploited or brainwashed by criminals, you need to recognize these risk factors to avoid falling into their traps and make smart decisions. Among these elements that can increase the likelihood of exploitation are:

- Lack of Experience: Teenagers may be more vulnerable to financial crimes due to their lack of life experience and awareness of potential risks. They may be easily influenced by peers or older people who exploit their naivety.

- Desire for Independence: As teenagers seek independence and autonomy, they may be drawn to illegal opportunities that promise quick and easy money.

- Online Presence: With the increased use of social media and the internet, teenagers may be vulnerable to online scams and fraudulent schemes that target their online activities.

- Lack of Financial Literacy: Many teenagers need basic financial literacy skills, making them vulnerable to manipulation and deception by those more familiar with financial systems.

- Peer Pressure: To fit in and be accepted by their peers, some teenagers may engage in illegal activities, including financial crimes, to gain respect or popularity within their social circles.

- Financial Stress: Teenagers from economically disadvantaged families may experience financial stress, making them more vulnerable to offers of easy money through illegal means.

- Social Life: Teenagers may encounter individuals involved in criminal activities or extremist ideologies in some cases, leading them down the path of illegal behaviour.

- Lack of Guidance: A lack of parental or adult guidance can leave teenagers without appropriate role models or mentors to help them navigate complex financial situations.

- Misguided Ambitions: Some teenagers may be swayed by the allure of wealth and success depicted in the media or pop culture, leading them to pursue illegal means to achieve their goals.

Some teenagers, feeling unstoppable and not worried about what might go wrong, might find themselves attracted to risky or even illegal activities. This daring curiosity could be a way for them to explore the world on their terms, sometimes going against what most people think is right or normal. However, it's crucial to remember that this could end tragically.

THE OBJECTIVE

Let us discuss something that might not be on your mind daily, but it's essential to know. It may sound like the least exciting topic, but understanding why financial crimes matter to you as a teenager is super important. So, let's dive in!

- Keep Yourself Safe: Financial crimes can directly impact your safety. Scammers, fraudsters, and identity thieves are out there, and knowing how to protect yourself from their tricks will keep your money and personal information secure.

- Your Money Matters: Knowing how to safeguard your assets from potential crimes is vital as you start earning money or receiving financial gifts. It's your hard-earned cash, and you want to ensure it stays safe.

- Build Trusting Relationships: Trust is the foundation of any good relationship, including money. Understanding financial crimes will help you make smart choices and build trust with others.

- Stay Out of Trouble: Involvement in financial crimes can lead to legal consequences, like fines or even jail time. Avoiding these situations will keep you out of trouble and protect your future opportunities.

- Make Ethical Choices: Learning about financial crimes helps you develop solid ethical decision-making skills.

- Protect Your Family: Your financial choices can impact your family too. By being aware of financial crimes, you can protect them from scams or frauds that might target you.

- Secure Your Future: Financial crimes can damage your reputation and future chances for school, jobs, and more. So, staying informed and making smart choices will help you achieve your dreams.

- Be Part of a Safer Society: Understanding and preventing financial crimes makes the world safer for everyone. By knowing more, you can help create a trustworthy financial environment.

- Take Charge of Your Finances: Knowledge is power! Learning about financial crimes empowers you to make intelligent decisions and not rely on others to handle your money.

- Become a Money Pro: Knowing about financial crimes means becoming financially savvy. The more you understand scams and fraudulent activities, the better you manage your money.

- Online Safety Matters: Many financial crimes happen online so understanding cybersecurity will protect your personal and financial information.

- Think for Yourself: Understanding financial crimes encourages you to think critically. Be skeptical of suspicious offers and research before making any financial decisions.

 So, there you have it – why financial crimes matter to you, and I hope this little chat has been eye-opening and you'll take this knowledge with you as you journey through life.

 By being informed and making wise choices, you can protect yourself, your loved ones, and your future. Stay smart, stay safe, and remember – you've got the power to make a difference!

SECTION TWO:
THE ESCAPE

This is an eye-opening section, where we venture into the depths of illegal activities that fuel the darker aspects of our society. From crimes that yield substantial profits while eluding justice to intricate schemes designed to obscure ill-gotten gains, we are about to expose the hidden truths behind these criminal operations.

Financial crimes come in diverse forms, and they extend far beyond mere monetary transactions. They inflict harm upon individuals, communities, and entire societies. To safeguard our present and future well-being, it is vital to comprehend the origins and implications of these illicit practices. By delving into the motives behind money laundering and navigating the ominous world of terrorist financing, we can equip ourselves with the knowledge to combat such wrongdoings effectively.

Within the following pages, we will explore the intricacies of moving and cleansing money, spanning across conventional financial channels, digital currencies, and even underground networks. Armed with insights into identifying the telltale signs of money laundering and understanding how criminals exploit vulnerabilities, we can thwart their illicit activities.

In the battle against financial crimes, knowledge becomes our most potent weapon. Together, we embark on this illuminating journey, driven by our unwavering passion for justice and the collective desire to create positive change. As we delve deeper, we will emerge equipped with the understanding needed to fortify our communities against the malevolence of financial crime.

CHAPTER THREE:
THE LAUNDRY

We may have already touched base on this devilish crime. I consider this crime to be the mother of all crimes! Why? Because children, when they escape, they run to their mother; in a world that fights and condemns financial crimes and illicit funds, every criminal need money laundry. In this chapter we will delve into the world of money laundering, its stages, and the main players.

THE DEFINITION OF MONEY LAUNDERING

Money laundering is a process through which individuals or organizations disguise the origins of illicitly obtained funds to make them appear legitimate. It involves a series of complex transactions and financial maneuvers designed to obscure the true source of the money and create the impression that it comes from legitimate sources. In other words, money laundering is a sinister financial crime that operates in the shadows, camouflaging the roots of unlawfully acquired funds to present them as lawful earnings. It's like a deceptive menu where the ingredients are masked to serve up a palatable dish of legitimacy. This illicit practice involves a web of intricate transactions and financial maneuvers that are strategically woven together to veil the true origin of the money. The goal? To conjure the illusion that these funds are clean and derived from lawful activities.

As a global predicament, money laundering poses a substantial threat to economies and societies. According to the United Nations Office on Drugs and Crime (UNODC), it's estimated that up to 5% of the world's GDP, roughly $2.6 trillion, is involved in money laundering annually. This staggering figure illustrates the sheer scale of the issue and how deeply it's woven into the fabric of the financial world.

One of the most shocking aspects of money laundering is the involvement of seemingly reputable institutions and individua.

From banks and financial institutions unwittingly or knowingly facilitating the process to professionals such as lawyers, accountants, and real estate agents aiding in creating the facade, it's a web that spans across sectors. The Panama Papers leak, which exposed the involvement of various politicians, celebrities, and business moguls in offshore tax havens, is a prime example of how money laundering can reach the highest echelons of society.

Another notable scandal is the case of the 1MDB scandal in Malaysia, where billions of dollars were embezzled from a state investment fund. This money was subsequently laundered through a complex web of transactions involving luxury real estate, art, and even the funding of Hollywood movies.

As authorities continue to grapple with this menace, understanding the nuances of money laundering is paramount. From smurfing and structuring to trade-based laundering, the perpetrators employ a range of techniques to launder money. By staying informed about the evolving landscape of this crime, we can collectively work towards dismantling its intricate mechanisms and safeguarding the integrity of our financial systems.

MONEY LAUNDERING STAGES

Criminals engage in the practice of money laundering, which is a form of financial deception that involves falsifying transactions and accounts to transform "dirty" money into assets that give the appearance of being legitimate. To conceal the illegal origins of their income, criminals engage in a meticulously choreographed performance of deception throughout the placement, layering, and integration stages of the process.

Placement

During the placement stage, those who launder money put their focus on legally channeling the profits of their illicit activities into the legal financial system. They frequently engage in less substantial business dealings to conceal their activities from the watchful eyes of law enforcement and to avoid arousing suspicion.

These activities may include depositing significant sums of money into several different bank accounts, making expensive purchases such as jewelry or luxury automobiles, or even funneling the money through casinos.

By combining dirty money with clean money, this gives the impression that the dirty money is legitimate. For instance, a criminal might put money that they obtained from the sale of drugs into the bank account of a made-up company.

Layering

The layering phase is where the intricate dance of deception gets its start. Those who launder money create a complex series of transactions that serve as smokescreens, making it difficult for anyone to determine the original source of the funds.

They might move money from one account to another, make transfers across international borders, and engage in complex stock trading. To further muddle the paper trail, it is common practice to use offshore accounts, shell companies, and trusts. This practice is widespread.

By utilizing these tactics, the goal is to render fruitless any investigation into the origin of the funds. Imagine a criminal moving money from one offshore account to another, then routing it through several reputable companies before reintroducing it to the legitimate economy. This would be an example of money laundering.

Integration

During the integration stage, dirty cash sneaks its way into the legitimate economy without being discovered. Those who launder money accomplish this goal by investing the funds in companies, properties, or other types of assets. They may create projects that give the appearance of being legitimate and then fund them with the illegal funds, which would effectively legitimize what they are doing.

At this point, the transformation of shady financial assets into respectable holdings is complete. For instance, a criminal could use money that has been laundered to buy commercial real estate, which would then generate what gives the appearance of being legal rental income.

It is worth mentioning that the criminals who commit the original crimes are not always the ones who launder their proceeds. Criminals may seek professional assistance to launder their illicit proceeds; those assistants can be third party individuals or existing businesses. That's why the crime that has produced illicit gains and money laundering are considered two different crimes.

THE CONSEQUENCES

Money laundering is bad for the world because it ruins societies from the inside out. It messes up real economies and makes inequality worse by taking money away from important public services. By giving criminals money that can't be tracked, it makes organized crime, human trafficking, and drug distribution easier. This makes communities less safe and less healthy.

This illegal practice destroys faith in fairness and justice by destroying trust in financial systems and institutions. Also, money laundering makes it possible for illegal activities to keep going, which slows down social progress by keeping cycles of violence and exploitation going. Getting rid of this threat is important if we want the world to be fair and safe.

It occurs on a staggeringly large scale. The United Nations Office on Drugs and Crime (UNODC) estimates that annually, money laundering accounts for somewhere in the range of 2% to 5% of global GDP, which translates to approximately

$800 billion to $2 trillion. This massive flow of illegal money undermines economies, supports criminal activity, and poses a threat to national security.

REAL CASES

In the infamous "Russian Laundromat" case, criminals used a network of businesses to smuggle $20 billion out of Russia and into the West while passing it off as ordinary business transactions. This massive operation to launder money involved participation from several different nations and financial institutions.

Another well-known instance, known as the "Troika Laundromat," involved a massive scheme to launder money that involved the movement of more than $4.8 billion through a complex network of front companies and offshore accounts. The funds were utilized for the purchase of luxurious goods and the purchase of expensive real estate investments.

Due to the sophistication and complexity of the schemes, the criminals in both instances were able to successfully launder billions of dollars before the authorities were able to figure out the truth.

In a nutshell, money laundering is an intricate process that requires complex transactions, deception, and the manipulation of various aspects of the financial system.

The stages of placing, layering, and integrating work in concert to conceal the origin of illegal funds and create the impression that the transaction is legitimate. It is essential to have a solid understanding of the mechanisms behind money laundering to continue the fight against financial crime and to keep the global economy fair and transparent.

CHAPTER FOUR: THE NEED FOR LAUNDERING

Addressing a frequently asked question, the ensuing pages delve into the motives behind criminals' engagement in money laundering and their inclination towards utilizing official financial systems.

DISGUISING THE SOURCE: CREATING THE APPEARANCE OF LEGITIMACY.

Money laundering is a complex process that criminals use to disguise the tainted origins of their illegally obtained funds. This intricate strategy entails channeling ill-gotten gains through seemingly lawful channels, such as shell companies or offshore accounts, to conceal any links to criminal activities. This maneuver acts as a smokescreen, concealing the true nature of the money trail and making it difficult for law enforcement and financial watchdogs to trace the illicit funds back to their criminal origins. At its heart, the process of concealing the source of funds entails a meticulously calculated series of transactions, each designed to separate the money from its criminal origins. These transactions frequently involve transfers between multiple accounts, various financial institutions, and, in some cases, across international borders.

Money launderers hope to confuse and complicate the paper trail in this way, making it extremely difficult for investigators to unravel the web of deceit.

FUNDING CRIMINAL ACTIVITIES: FEEDING THE BEAST

Laundering money serves a dual purpose for criminals: it not only enables them to conceal the origins of their ill-gotten gains, but it also provides a convenient mechanism to finance and expand their ongoing criminal enterprises. In other words, money laundering is a tool that serves a dual purpose for criminals. After illegal funds have been successfully laundered and transformed into assets that give the appearance of being legitimate, these assets can then be reintroduced into the criminal ecosystem to fuel additional illegal activities. This sneaky practice of repurposing clean money to fund illegal activities results in the formation of a vicious cycle of criminal activity that can have extremely negative repercussions for society.

To provide an example, consider the following scenario involving drug traffickers: Once they have "cleaned" the profits from their illegal drug trade, they can put those funds towards the purchase of even more illegal drugs. This not only allows them to continue their illegal activities but also helps replenish their stock. As a result, the market will continue to receive a consistent supply of drugs.

In addition, this cycle magnifies the negative effects that illegal activities have on society.

In the case of drug trafficking, for example, the accessibility of drugs purchased with money that has been laundered can contribute to an increase in the prevalence of addiction and the criminal activities that are associated with it. This not only ensures that the initial criminal act will continue to have repercussions for affected communities, but it also makes the resulting social and economic problems even more severe.

ENJOYING GAINS: TASTING THE HONEY

Money laundering allows criminals to reap the benefits of their illegal activities while avoiding detection and suspicion. One of the primary motivations for money laundering is to convert "dirty" money that has been tainted by its criminal origins into assets that appear legitimate and can be freely enjoyed.

Criminals accomplish this by strategically investing their laundered funds in tangible assets of significant value, such as prime real estate, luxury automobiles, fine art, and other high-end goods. These assets not only serve as a means of safeguarding their wealth, but also as status symbols that exude success and prosperity.

Criminals hope to divert attention away from their illegal activities by publicly displaying these opulent possessions, making it difficult for law enforcement or regulatory authorities to connect them to criminal behaviour. This practice of concealing the source of funds through ostentatious displays of wealth can be especially appealing to criminals seeking to maintain a veneer of legitimacy in society.

The ability to live extravagantly while remaining unnoticed by law enforcement can give criminals a sense of invincibility and encourage them to continue their illegal activities. This dynamic emphasises the difficulty of investigating and prosecuting money laundering cases. Detecting the links between ill-gotten gains and extravagant purchases necessitates a meticulous examination of financial transactions, asset ownership, and connections to criminal networks.

GETTING PERMANENT ACCESS & WHITENING THE COLLARS

Money laundering gives criminals access to a variety of financial services and opportunities that they would not otherwise have access to by giving them the appearance of legitimacy. Criminals can infiltrate the legal economy and operate legally, albeit covertly, by successfully hiding the sources of their illicit gains.

Having the ability to establish a spotless financial identity is one of the main benefits of money laundering. Criminals can open bank accounts, obtain credit lines, and carry out investment activities using laundered money without paying attention to themselves, simply because they have a good reputation.

For instance, criminals may use laundered funds to buy stocks, make real estate investments, or even launch businesses that appear to be legitimate. Through these activities, criminals can not only earn money but also blend in with legitimate business operations. They can engage in business dealings and partnerships that are identical to those of law-abiding citizens by operating under the guise of apparent legality.

Criminals can assume two identities: one as a law-abiding citizen and the other as a participant in illegal businesses thanks to their ability to engage in legal economic activity while hiding their criminal affiliations.

This duality makes it more difficult to find and catch criminals because their legal activities serve as a cover for their illegal ones. The fuzziness of the lines separating legal and illegal activities emphasises how crucial financial institutions are to stopping money laundering.

To stop criminals from using banks to hide their stolen money, rules called 'know-your-customer' (KYC) and 'anti-money laundering' (AML) are really important. Think of it like a security check at an amusement park - the banks have to know who's coming in and what they're doing. By being really careful and watching for anything strange, they can make it harder for bad guys to use the system for their own gains. It's like a big game of hide-and-seek, where criminals try to mix in their stolen money with the regular money. These rules help make sure the bad money doesn't get mixed in, making it easier for the police to figure out what's legal and what's not.

THE GREEN ISOLATION: FORTIFYING SAFEGUARDS

Imagine a criminal who has a lot of stolen money. They're always worried that someone might find out about their hidden treasure, so they come up with a clever way to protect it. This is called the 'Green Isolation' strategy, something I've been researching and understanding.

Think of it like a game of hide-and-seek with money. The criminals take some of the stolen money and hide it extra carefully. They wash it, mix it with other money, and wash it again, again and again, until it's so clean it looks like they earned it legally. It's like washing a red shirt with white ones until it turns pink, then washing it with pink shirts until it turns white. This 'green isolated' money is supposed to be so well-hidden that no one can find it, even if they know about the other stolen money.

Criminals like to have this 'extra secure' money because it makes them feel safe. If something goes wrong and they get caught, they can always point to this clean money and say, 'See? I earned this legally!' It's like having a secret stash of candy that no one knows about, just in case you get hungry later.

But here's the cool part: the good guys are getting better and better at finding this hidden money. They're like detectives with special tools and tricks to find clues, even when the criminals think they've hidden them well. They can peel back the layers, like an onion, and find the stolen money, no matter how well it's been hidden.

So, even though criminals try to be super clever and sneaky, the good guys are always getting smarter too. The 'Green Isolation' strategy might seem like an unbreakable code, but it's not. It's just another puzzle to solve in the fight against financial crimes, and understanding it helps make the world a safer place.

SHAPING PERCEPTION: CRIMINALS & THE ART OF LONG-TERM DECEPTION

Imagine playing a really long game of hide-and-seek where you don't just hide once; you keep moving around, changing your hiding spots and even your appearance. Financial criminals do something similar, but they're hiding their stolen money.

These people are like master artists, painting a picture that makes them look like regular, law-abiding citizens. It's like they're wearing a disguise, and they want to make sure nobody ever recognizes them for what they really are.

Here's how they do it:

- Slow and Steady Wins the Race: They don't just dump all their stolen money into the bank. They take their time, add a little bit here and there, make it look like it's coming from legal sources. It's like a chameleon blending into its surroundings. Slowly but surely, they become part of the scenery.

- Pattern Play: By repeatedly doing the same thing, these criminals make their illegal activities seem normal. Think of it like hearing a strange noise at night. At first, it might scare you, but if it happens every night, you'll get used to it. That's what they're aiming for.

- The Shell Game: They'll use fake companies and complicated networks to make tracking the money really hard. Imagine trying to follow a ball under one of three cups as someone shuffles them around super fast. It's confusing, right?

- The Long Con: This is a patient game. They're willing to spend years, even decades, looking like good guys. They're betting that if they keep up the act long enough, even the sharpest minds will start to see them as legit.

But here's the thing: they're not invincible. Even though they try super hard to look normal, the good guys—like detectives, banks, and government agencies—are always learning new ways to spot them. It's like a never-ending game of cat and mouse, where both sides are always trying to outsmart each other. In the end, it's about understanding that money isn't just something you spend. It's a tool, and like any tool, it can be used for good or bad. By understanding how the bad guys use it, we can all become more aware and protect ourselves from being caught up in their games.

THE SAFEST SAFE: CRIMINALS AND THE
OFFICIAL FINANCIAL SYSTEM.

Imagine you're playing a video game where the rules are set up to make sure everyone plays fair. But then, some players find a way to use those very rules to cheat without getting caught. Sounds crazy, right? But in the world of money and finance, this is exactly what's happening.

Here's how it works:

A Secure Base: Criminals want to keep their stolen money safe, just like you might keep your hard-earned gaming points safe. Surprisingly, they often hide it in regular banks and financial systems. Why? Because these places have lots of rules to protect money. It's like hiding something right under everyone's nose.

- Moving Money with Ease: The banks and financial systems we use every day to save, spend, and send money can also be used by criminals. They can move their stolen money around, invest it, and even spend it, all while making it look legit. It's like putting on a disguise and acting like a law-abiding citizen.

- Blending In: By mixing their stolen money with legal money, criminals create a confusing trail that's hard to follow. Imagine trying to find a specific piece of a jigsaw puzzle in a room filled with thousands of other puzzles. It's pretty tough, right?

- Going Global: The world's banks are connected, so money can move from one country to another quickly. Criminals use this to their advantage, sending money all over the place to make it even harder to trace back to them.

But, guess what? They don't always get away with it.

The people who protect our financial system are like super-smart detectives. They keep learning new ways to spot the bad guys, even when they're hiding in plain sight.

So, what's the big lesson here? Even something as solid and trustworthy as a bank can be tricked if the criminals are clever enough. But the good guys are always learning and adapting, too. It's a high-stakes game of cat and mouse, with lots of twists and turns. And it shows that nothing's ever completely black or white, especially when it comes to money. Sometimes the bad guys use the good guys' tools, but that doesn't mean they always win.

CERTIFICATION OF CLEAN MONEY: MONEY LAUNDERERS' APPROACH TO REPUTABLE FINANCIAL SYSTEMS.

Imagine you've created an incredibly realistic painting of a famous superhero. It's so good that everyone believes it's a genuine piece of art by a renowned artist. They don't know that it's your creation, and it hangs in a well-known art gallery. The fact that it's in that gallery gives it an unspoken stamp of approval. People see it there, assume it's legit, and never question its authenticity.

Now, let's connect this to the world of money laundering:

- The Silent Approval: When criminals put their illegal money into well-known banks or financial systems, they're like that painting hanging in the art gallery. The very act of being in a place known for trust and respectability makes people think it's legitimate. It's like saying, "If it's here, it must be real."

- The Disguise: The money is hidden in plain sight, like a fake painting in a gallery. It's mixed with real, legal money, so it's hard to tell what's what. The bad guys dress up their stolen funds, making them look all fancy and proper, so nobody questions where it came from.

- The Unspoken Validation: The banks don't know they've been tricked, so they treat the money like any other funds. This lack of suspicion acts as a silent nod, a secret thumbs-up that the criminals have succeeded in fooling everyone. It's like the gallery owner complimenting the fake painting, thinking it's a masterpiece.

- The Irony: Here's where it gets interesting. The criminals are seeking approval from the very places designed to catch them! It's a risky game, but the rewards are high. If they pull it off, they haven't just hidden their money; they've turned it into something that everyone accepts as real and good.

So what's the takeaway? It's a weird, upside-down world where the bad guys are seeking approval from the good guys without them even knowing. They're turning something bad into something that looks good, all within the very system designed to stop them. This game of financial hide-and-seek shows how clever and twisted the world of money laundering can be. It's not just about hiding; it's about transforming and seeking a silent, unspoken stamp of approval. And like a painting that's too good to be true, sometimes it's the things right under our noses that are the hardest to see.

CHAPTER FIVE: THE TERRORIST FINANCING

The financing of terrorism is a particularly dark aspect of the landscape of financial criminality. It is a symbol of the murky connection that exists between illegal funds and acts of violence that undermine the very foundation of international safety.

This chapter reveals a chilling reality where funds are manipulated and channeled to enable destructive agendas, and it does so by illuminating the intricate web of connections that fuel terrorism through financial means.

As we delve deeper into the subject of terrorist financing, we are discovering that the activities involved go beyond simple monetary transactions and become the driving force behind both violent extremist ideology and acts of terrorism.

Terrorist organisations depend on a sophisticated network of financial support to sustain their malicious activities. This support encompasses various aspects, such as recruitment and training, spreading their ideologies, and carrying out deadly attacks. Funds play a crucial role in the operations of these groups, enabling them to operate covertly and extend their influence with severe consequences.

Recruitment efforts necessitate financial support in order to entice vulnerable individuals by offering them monetary rewards or assistance for their families.

After being recruited, members require training and resources, all of which necessitate funding for weapons, equipment, safehouses, and travel expenses.

They take advantage of modern communication channels to disseminate their ideologies and recruit sympathizers. This requires allocating resources for creating propaganda materials, developing websites, and launching social media campaigns.

The act of disseminating information helps to increase their influence internationally, making financial support crucial for maintaining a global presence. In addition, carrying out acts of terror requires careful planning, which necessitates financial support for various aspects such as logistics, transportation, surveillance, and coordination.

Terrorist organisations engage in a wide range of activities that impose a significant financial burden, requiring a continuous flow of funds to support their operations.

Financial support for various activities is typically obtained from a combination of legitimate sources, such as donations from sympathizers or charitable organisations, as well as illicit means like drug trafficking, arms smuggling, and extortion.

Consider the following aspects:

- Distinct Flow of Funds: Unlike the circular nature of money laundering, funds in terrorist financing follow a one-way trajectory. While money laundering often involves complex cycles, the funds utilized for terrorist financing have a singular purpose and direction.

- Varied Actors: The spectrum of those involved in terrorist financing ranges from criminals to individuals and legitimate entities. This diverse range of actors underscores the challenge in identifying and countering such activities, as the financiers can operate under different guises.

- Accumulation Through Aggregation: A distinctive characteristic of terrorist financing is the accumulation of funds through incremental contributions. Even small amounts can be amassed and channeled into a consolidated pool, making it more challenging to trace the origins and movements of the funds.

- Preference for Underground Systems: Terrorist financiers often gravitate toward underground financial systems to evade detection. These covert channels provide a cloak of secrecy that hampers law enforcement efforts to track and disrupt their funding sources.

THE IMPACT

The complex web of terrorism financing has far reached implications that go beyond the immediate financial sphere. The following discussion explores the ways in which the financing of terrorism contributes to the worsening of global instability, the creation of a sense of insecurity, and the tragic loss of innocent lives.

- Instability and insecurity on a global scale: the funds that are funneled towards terrorist organisations provide the fuel for their activities, which frequently involve acts of violence, destruction, and anarchy.

Supporters of these groups unintentionally contribute to the destabilization of regions and countries by providing financial support to these organisations. The instability that ensues slows down social and economic development, wreaks havoc on governance structures, and creates an atmosphere that is fertile ground for the growth of extremist ideologies.

- Loss of Life The loss of countless lives is perhaps the most heartbreaking consequence of terrorist financing. The provision of funds to terrorist organisations enables those organisations to plan and carry out attacks that result in casualties and injuries.

The majority of the suffering caused by these acts of violence is borne by innocent civilians who are either caught in the crossfire or intentionally targeted. The amount of suffering, trauma, and grief that the affected families and communities have gone through is incalculable.

CHAPTER SIX: THE FUNNELS AND CHANNELS

In the intricate world of financial crimes, the methods used to move and conceal illicit funds can be as diverse as they are complex. Criminals and illicit actors continually innovate ways to blur the lines between lawful and unlawful activities, making the detection and prevention of these activities a challenging endeavor.

This chapter delves into a crucial aspect of money laundering and terrorist financing: the utilization of "funnels" and "channels."

These terms might evoke images of pathways and conduits, and indeed, they aptly capture the essence of how funds are maneuvered and obscured in the realm of financial wrongdoing. Understanding the concepts of funnels and channels is akin to unlocking the intricate mechanics of financial crimes.

Money Laundering Funnels

Imagine baking a cake and using a funnel to pour the batter into different shapes. That's what criminals do with their illegal money, except they're using "funnels" to pour it into different forms that make it look clean.

Here's how it works:

- Mixing It Up: Criminals start by mixing their dirty money with clean money. It's like blending various ingredients to make a cake mix.

- Pouring Through Different Shapes: Then, they pour the money into different bank accounts, companies, or investments, just like you'd pour the batter into various cake pans.

- Cooking It Slowly: Through different stages, they slowly "cook" the money, making it harder to tell where it came from. It's like baking the cake at different temperatures to get the perfect texture.

- Decorating with Fancy Toppings: Finally, they use the laundered money to buy luxury things like mansions or fancy cars. It's like putting frosting and sprinkles on the cake to make it look appealing.

Money Laundering Channels

Now, think about different pipes or channels that water can flow through. Money launderers use "channels" to move their dirty money through various routes, making it look like ordinary money.

Here's how that works:

- Choosing the Right Pipes: Criminals pick different channels or "pipes" like shell companies, online platforms, or real estate to move their money.

- Adjusting the Flow: They control how fast or slow the money goes through the channels, like adjusting the flow of water through a hose.

- Making It Look Normal: By using many different paths, they make the money look like it's just normal everyday cash, just like how water flowing through pipes is a usual sight.

- Turning Dirty into Clean: In the end, the dirty money comes out the other side looking all clean and legal, just like water flowing out of a faucet.

Why Understanding Funnels and Channels Matters?

These tricky methods are like a magician's secrets, making money disappear here and reappear there. But unlike magic tricks, these methods are used to hide real crimes and hurt real people.

Understanding how criminals use funnels and channels helps us figure out how to stop them. It's like learning the secrets behind a magician's tricks, so you can catch them out. By knowing what to look for, people who fight financial crimes can follow the money, uncover the secrets, and stop the bad guys.

MONEY LAUNDERING TYPOLOGIES

Money laundering typologies refer to various methods and techniques that criminals use to legitimize their illicitly obtained funds. These typologies are designed to obscure the origins of the money and make it appear as though it comes from legal sources.

They encompass a range of strategies, each tailored to exploit different vulnerabilities in financial systems and regulations.

By understanding these typologies, law enforcement and financial institutions can better detect and prevent money laundering activities. Some common money laundering typologies include:

TRADE-BASED MONEY LAUNDERING

Trade-Based Money Laundering (TBML) is a sophisticated method that criminals employ to disguise the origins of illicit funds by exploiting international trade transactions.

This typology capitalizes on the complexities of cross-border trade, involving the movement of goods and services between countries. By manipulating the pricing of these goods and services, criminals aim to create discrepancies in the recorded value of the trade, which in turn facilitates the movement of money without arousing suspicion. In the case of over-invoicing, criminals intentionally inflate the value of goods or services being traded. For example, if the actual value of a shipment is $100,000, they might invoice it as $150,000.

This overvaluation creates an apparent surplus of funds in the transaction, allowing the excess $50,000 to be moved across borders as part of the legitimate trade. The surplus can then be received by an associate or accomplice in another country.

Conversely, under-invoicing involves deliberately undervaluing the traded goods or services. In this scenario, if the shipment's actual value is $100,000, criminals might report it as $70,000. The remaining $30,000, which represents the difference between the actual value and the invoiced value, can be transferred secretly to another location.

TBML also includes the manipulation of quantity, quality, and even the description of the goods. Criminals might ship fewer goods than declared or substitute them with lower-value items. These alterations aim to create a facade of legitimate trade while siphoning off funds for illegal purposes.

This typology is particularly attractive to criminals due to the global nature of trade and the inherent complexities involved in tracking the movement of goods and funds across borders. Customs documents, invoices, and shipping records can be manipulated to obfuscate the true nature of the transactions.

Additionally, the involvement of multiple parties, such as exporters, importers, shipping companies, and financial institutions, further complicates the detection process.

The consequences of TBML are far-reaching, affecting not only financial institutions but also governments, economies, and the overall stability of trade systems. Law enforcement agencies and regulatory bodies worldwide are increasingly working to enhance their monitoring and detection capabilities to combat this form of money laundering.

To address TBML, collaborative efforts between financial institutions, trade authorities, and regulatory bodies are crucial.

parallelly, the Enhanced due diligence and transaction monitoring, as well as the use of advanced data analytics and technology, are essential in identifying suspicious trade activities and uncovering attempts to manipulate trade transactions for illicit gains.

SMURFING

Smurfing, or structuring, is like building a giant LEGO castle but using lots of different people and locations to place the individual LEGO bricks. Each brick represents a small amount of money, and the whole castle symbolizes the total sum of illegal money that criminals want to hide.

Here's how it works:

- Breaking It Down: Think of a big LEGO set as the illegal money that criminals want to build into something legit. They break the set down into individual pieces, or smaller amounts of money.

- Handing Out the Bricks: Just like in a giant LEGO project where lots of people might be involved in building something, criminals use different people, known as "Smurfs," to place each LEGO brick. These Smurfs might not even know they're building something illegal.

- Building in Different Places: These LEGO bricks (small amounts of money) are placed in different banks, businesses, or locations. It's like building different parts of the castle in different places to hide what's really being built.

- Connecting the Pieces: Eventually, all these individual LEGO bricks form a complete structure, and the criminals have successfully turned their illegal money into something that looks legal.

Why Is It Called "Smurfing"?

The name might remind you of the blue Smurfs cartoon characters. Imagine each Smurf being given a little task, not knowing they're all working together to build something big. It's the same in money laundering: lots of people handle small amounts of money, not knowing they're part of a bigger criminal scheme.

Why Is Smurfing a Problem?

Just like building a massive LEGO castle without anyone noticing would be quite a feat, smurfing is a sneaky way to do something big without getting caught. It makes it hard for banks and police to notice because everything looks like normal, everyday transactions.

How Can We Stop Smurfing?

Stopping smurfing is like trying to catch all those individual LEGO bricks being placed around different locations. It requires smart detectives who can notice patterns, like realizing that a bunch of random LEGO pieces are actually part of the same set. Banks and law enforcement agencies use special tools to track and connect these transactions, looking for clues that something isn't quite right.

Money Mules and the Risk to Teens

In the complex world of financial crimes, there are many ways that criminals try to hide their activities. One method is through the use of "money mules. Money mules are individuals who, knowingly or unknowingly, transfer illegal funds on behalf of others. Unfortunately, teenagers, with their limited experience and understanding of financial systems, can become targets and be used as money mules.

How Teens Can Become Money Mules?

- Online Lures: Many teenagers are active online and may come across seemingly legitimate job offers that promise quick and easy money. These offers could be scams designed to recruit money mules.

- Peer Pressure: Friends or acquaintances involved in these activities might persuade others to participate, playing down the risks and emphasizing the rewards.

- Lack of Awareness: Teenagers may not fully understand the legal implications of their actions, which makes them susceptible targets for criminals looking for mules.

CASH SMUGGLING

A method of money laundering known as "cash smuggling" depends on the actual movement of cash across international borders. To conceal the movement of illicit funds, criminals take advantage of the difficulties in detecting and tracking physical currency. This technique makes it more challenging for law enforcement to track the movement of illicit funds by hiding large sums of money inside of a variety of items, including luggage, vehicles, and shipments of goods. Cash smuggling's main objective is to take advantage of how difficult it is for border and customs officials to locate hidden cash. Physical currency doesn't have the same level of traceability as electronic transactions, which can leave a digital trail. Criminals take advantage of this hole by coming up with clever ways to conceal money and carry it across borders covertly.

To facilitate cash smuggling, it's common practice to divide the illegal funds into smaller, more manageable sums. These smaller sums of money are then cleverly concealed inside commonplace items like clothing, electronics, or household goods. Criminals may stuff cash between layers of merchandise in shipping containers, conceal it in the compartments of electronic devices, or sew it into the lining of clothing.

Vehicles are important in the smuggling of cash as well. In order to conceal large amounts of cash, thieves may modify the interior of cars, trucks, or even commercial vehicles to add secret compartments. Without sophisticated inspection methods or specially trained personnel, it may not be easy to find these concealed compartments.

In more complex situations, criminals use shipments of legal goods as a cover to move money that isn't theirs. It is challenging for authorities to distinguish between legitimate and illegitimate shipments because cash can be concealed within cargo containers along with legal goods.

By concealing the money among items that appear to be harmless, this tactic makes it more difficult to spot suspicious activity.

It is clear that fighting cash smuggling is difficult. During routine inspections, traditional border control measures frequently cause trouble finding hidden cash. Criminals constantly come up with new ways to hide money, so law enforcement agencies must continue to be flexible and creative in their methods.

Governments and border security organisations have reacted by putting money into cutting-edge scanning technology, like X-ray scanners and sniffer dogs trained to find hidden cash.

These instruments can assist in locating anomalies in a variety of objects and automobiles, possibly leading to the discovery of hidden funds. International cooperation is also essential because criminals frequently use gaps in border security to transfer money between countries.

Physical transportation of cash across borders is another method criminals use to launder money. It can involve hiding money in various forms, such as within luggage, vehicles, or shipments.

REAL ESTATE INVESTMENTS

Investing in real estate has become a popular option for criminals looking to legalize their illicit gains. This strategy entails purchasing tangible assets, like properties, with money that was obtained illegally in order to conceal the source of the funds and perhaps make future profits. Real estate is alluring because it can give criminals a veneer of legitimacy and a chance to advance their careers.

Due to the inherent complexity of the real estate market and the numerous ways in which transactions can be set up, criminals prefer to invest in real estate. They can inject their illicit funds into the legal economy by buying expensive properties, positioning themselves to gain from rising property values. Real estate can absorb sizable sums of money without raising suspicion, which is one of its main benefits. It is challenging for authorities to track down the source of the funds when criminals use a combination of cash and loans to buy properties across the globe.

The property market also frequently uses intricate ownership structures, such as trusts or shell companies, which can further obscure the identity of the ultimate beneficiary.

In order to increase their chances of making sizable profits when they decide to sell, money launderers frequently look for properties in prime locations with high appreciation potential.

Due to the constant demand for such assets, properties in prestigious areas also have the advantage of being simpler to sell without arousing suspicion. Criminals may manipulate property values through phony appraisals, inflating the value of the assets they have purchased, further complicating the tracking of illicit funds. This artificially inflates the investment's apparent value, enabling criminals to justify spending more money than they did to buy the property. Sometimes, criminals will carry out a number of real estate deals to leave a paper trail that seems legitimate.

For instance, they might buy property with illegal money and then "sell" it to another party for a higher sum, appearing to be conducting a legal business. The practice of "flipping" properties can give the appearance of legitimate income streams and capital gains.

Although investing in real estate might seem like the ideal way to launder money, regulatory bodies and law enforcement organisations are stepping up their oversight.

The use of the real estate sector for illegal purposes is being curbed through increased scrutiny of high-value transactions, improved due diligence, and regulations that demand transparency in property transactions.

Imagine you've got a bunch of dirty clothes that you don't want anyone to know about, but you also want them clean and wearable. What do you do? You find a way to wash them without anyone noticing. Criminals do the same thing with their "dirty" money. Here's how:

1. Choosing Real Estate as a Washing Machine

Buying properties like houses, apartments, or land is like choosing a washing machine to clean their dirty money. Why real estate?

Size: Real estate can handle big amounts of money without looking weird.

Complicated Settings: The property market has many options and ways to set up purchases, making it easier to hide what's really happening.

Popularity: Real estate is attractive, and criminals can pretend to be legitimate investors or businesspeople.

2. The Laundry Process: Buying Properties

Criminals buy properties with their illegal money, like throwing dirty clothes into the washing machine.

Mixing Water and Detergent: They use a combination of cash and loans, buying properties in different places to mix everything up and make it hard to trace.

Using Different Washing Programs: They might set up complex ownership structures, like trusts or fake companies, to hide who really owns the property.

3. Drying and Folding: Increasing Value and Selling

Once they own the properties, criminals might try to increase their value or sell them in tricky ways:

Fluffing the Clothes: By manipulating property values and creating fake appraisals, they make their investments look more valuable than they really are.

Folding and Stacking: They may "flip" properties, buying and selling them to make their money look clean and legal, like neatly folding and stacking clothes.

4. Wearing the Clean Clothes: Enjoying the Benefits

Once the money is cleaned through real estate, criminals can enjoy their new "clothes." They might make profits, live in luxurious homes, or even build a fake business reputation.

Luckily, there are people watching out for these shady laundry activities. Authorities, banks, and regulators are like laundry inspectors, looking for unusual washing patterns. They use rules and careful examination to catch criminals and stop them from using the real estate market to clean their dirty money.

ONLINE PAYMENT SYSTEMS

Criminals have realised the potential of online payment systems as a tool for money laundering in the ever-changing world of financial crimes. A wide range of platforms and channels are available in the digital world for the movement, concealment, and legitimization of illicit funds. Due to their inherent characteristics of anonymity, speed, and global reach, online payment systems, while intended to facilitate legitimate financial transactions, have unintentionally turned into a haven for money launderers.

The allure of online payment systems lies in their capacity to give financial transactions a fictitious veil of invisibility. It is nearly impossible for authorities to determine who the true owners of the funds are because these platforms frequently allow users to open accounts using fictitious names or credentials. Further complicating efforts to track down and seize illicit funds is the speed at which digital transactions allow criminals to send large sums of money across borders in a matter of seconds.

Money laundering has given cryptocurrency, a subset of online payment systems, much attention. Users of cryptocurrencies like Bitcoin enjoy a previously unheard-of level of anonymity thanks to their decentralized and pseudonymous nature. Criminals can take advantage of this feature by converting their illicit funds into cryptocurrency, using blockchain networks to conduct transactions that are inherently hard to track, and then exchanging the cryptocurrency back for fiat money in a location far from the original source.

Money launderers also frequently use prepaid cards and virtual money. You can load money onto these devices —often in small denominations—and use it to make purchases, send money, or withdraw cash.

Criminals can layer their funds through multiple transactions, taking advantage of the anonymity that these techniques offer, making it harder for authorities to determine the money's source and final destination.

Law enforcement organisations face more difficulties as a result of the internet's global reach. Criminals can carry out transactions from anywhere in the world by concealing their real location with virtual private networks (VPNs). Because of this, it is challenging for the authorities to establish their authority and coordinate their efforts to look into and prosecute cases of money laundering.

OFFSHORE ACCOUNTS

one strategy that criminals employ to evade detection and safeguard their ill-gotten gains is the utilization of offshore bank accounts and tax havens. These clandestine financial enclaves offer an appealing combination of secrecy, minimal regulatory scrutiny, and tax advantages, providing criminals with a haven to shield their illicit wealth from prying eyes.

Offshore accounts serve as a veil of secrecy, allowing criminals to obscure their financial activities from the watchful gaze of law enforcement agencies and financial institutions. These accounts often come with strict confidentiality provisions and legal protections that make it difficult for authorities to gain access to account information or transaction records. As a result, criminals can conduct their financial operations with a sense of impunity, confident that their activities remain hidden from view.

Tax havens, typically characterized by low or zero taxation and lenient financial regulations, attract money launderers seeking to minimize their tax liabilities and regulatory obligations. By funneling their illicit funds through these havens, criminals can effectively reduce the paper trail and audit trail associated with their transactions. This layer of financial opaqueness complicates efforts to trace the flow of funds, hampering investigations into money laundering activities.

The process of using offshore accounts to launder money often involves a complex web of transactions designed to obfuscate the origin of the funds further. Criminals may establish shell companies or trusts in tax havens, which serve as vehicles for moving and layering money. These entities can be controlled through nominee directors or shareholders, adding another layer of secrecy to the arrangement. Transactions between these entities can take convoluted paths, making it challenging for authorities to discern the true beneficiaries and purpose of the funds.

Offshore accounts and tax havens also enable criminals to access their laundered funds discreetly. With the use of encrypted communication and private banking services, they can manage and move their wealth remotely, often from the comfort of their own homes.

This level of convenience and privacy provides criminals with a significant advantage in maintaining control over their assets while avoiding exposure to potential risks.

let me put it in a more simple way:

1. Finding the Secret Island

Think of criminals like pirates who've stolen lots of treasure and now need to hide it from the authorities. Offshore bank accounts and tax havens are like secret treasure islands where they can hide their ill-gotten gains. Why do they like these islands?

- Hidden from View: These secret islands have lots of places to hide the treasure (money) and make it hard for the authorities to find it.

- Fewer Rules: The islands don't have many rules about what can and can't be done with the money, so the pirates (criminals) have more freedom.

- Lower Taxes: Pirates don't like paying taxes any more than the rest of us, and these islands don't charge many taxes, so the pirates keep more of their treasure.

2. Hiding the Treasure

The pirates have to be sneaky when hiding their treasure so no one finds it. Here's how they do it:

- Creating Fake Treasure Maps: Criminals create fake companies or trusts in these secret islands. It's like drawing fake treasure maps that lead to nowhere.

- Using Secret Agents: They might use other people (like nominee directors) to control the money without being seen. It's like having secret agents to bury and move the treasure.

- Making Confusing Trails: They move money in complicated ways so that anyone following the treasure trail gets lost.

3. Accessing the Hidden Treasure

Once the treasure is hidden, the pirates can access it whenever they want:

- Using Spy Gadgets: With encrypted communication and private banking, criminals can get to their money without leaving home. It's like using spy gadgets to keep an eye on their hidden treasure.

- Staying in Control: These secret islands give criminals a big advantage in controlling their treasure while staying hidden from the authorities.

GAMBLING

Casinos and other gambling venues become unwitting

platforms that criminals can use to conceal their illegal wealth. In order to obtain what appears to be legitimate funds, the process entails turning dirty money into gambling chips or using it to place bets and then cashing out winnings. This method of money laundering takes advantage of the difficulties faced by the gambling industry, where a sizable cash flow and the appearance of entertainment can hide the source of illegally obtained funds.

The convenience of moving and transforming large sums of money makes casinos attractive as a location for money laundering. Armed with their illegally obtained money, criminals enter a casino and turn it into gambling chips that they use to place bets. It can be difficult for investigators to distinguish between legal gambling and money-laundering schemes because the act of gambling acts as a smokescreen.

To legalize the proceeds of a variety of criminal activities, from drug trafficking to organized crime, criminal organisations frequently plan the use of gambling establishments. The procedure can be as simple as exchanging money for chips and then cashing out to make the money appear to be the result of gambling winnings. The original criminal source is effectively covered up by integrating the winnings into the legal financial system.

Casinos and other gambling establishments are desirable targets for money laundering due to their inherent allure. These places thrive in a buzzing atmosphere of thrills, big stakes, and secrecy. The sheer volume of transactions—both legal and illegal—that occur inside a casino makes it more difficult to distinguish between actual gamblers and those using the place to conduct illegal financial transactions.

Recent years have seen an increase in online gambling platforms, opening up new opportunities for money laundering. Without ever setting foot inside a real casino, thieves can easily transfer money through virtual platforms, place bets, and withdraw winnings. The fact that these transactions are digital increases the difficulty of identifying and stopping money laundering activities.

The gambling industry is now subject to more scrutiny and regulations as a result of efforts to stop money laundering. Anti-money laundering (AML) regulations are becoming more and more applicable to casinos and other gambling facilities, requiring them to implement stringent customer due diligence procedures and notify regulatory authorities of any suspicious transactions. The ever-evolving criminal tactics, though, put these safeguards to the test, calling for constant vigilance and collaboration between law enforcement and the gambling sector.

In conclusion, the use of casinos and gambling establishments as money-laundering funnels demonstrates how creative criminals can be when looking for ways to legalize their illegal gains. The combination of gambling excitement and criminal proceeds results in a convoluted web of transactions that is challenging to unravel. Vigilance and proactive regulatory efforts are still essential in preventing the use of gambling as a means of money laundering as the financial landscape changes.

Imagine being a detective in a glitzy casino filled with the sounds of slot machines, the excitement of card games, and the buzz of people enjoying a night out. Now, what if hidden among the legitimate gamblers were criminals using the casino to "clean" their stolen money? Here's how this tricky game plays out:

1. The Criminal's Game Plan

The Dirty Money Problem: Criminals have loads of money from bad things like stealing or drug dealing, but they can't spend it because people might find out where it came from.

The Casino Solution: Casinos love money, and people win and lose all the time. Criminals think, "Why not pretend our bad money is just gambling money?"

2. Playing the Game: How It Works?

Buying Chips with Dirty Money: The criminal walks into the

casino with a suitcase full of "dirty" money and buys lots of chips.

Gamble (Or Pretend To!): They play games or sometimes just pretend to, so it looks like they're a regular gambler.

Cashing Out Clean Money: At the end of the night, they cash in the chips and leave with "clean" money. Now it looks like they won it fairly, and nobody asks questions.

3. Why Casinos? The Perfect Playground

Excitement and Secrets: Casinos are exciting and full of secrets. Lots of money moves around, and no one notices a little more.

Online Playgrounds: With online casinos, criminals don't even need to leave home! They can play the same game online, making it even trickier to catch them.

ART AND ANTIQUE TRANSACTIONS

The art market emerges as an unexpected and alluring avenue for criminals to launder their illicit gains in the world of financial crime. This strategy entails the strategic purchase of priceless antiques or artwork, which are then sold again to conceal the funds' true source and to raise money for other illegal activities.

The use of the art market as a means of money laundering takes advantage of the distinctive features of the art world. Antiques and works of art have intrinsic value that frequently increases over time, making them appealing investment options. In order to move their contaminated funds through a complicated web of transactions, art dealers, galleries, and auction houses, criminals take advantage of this inherent value.

This strategy's central component is the use of illegal funds to buy pricey items. Criminals purchase antiques or works of art through transactions that on the surface might seem to be legal. Private sales, public auctions, and direct discussions with art dealers are all possible methods of acquiring these works. As the acquired works are incorporated into the art market, a veneer of legitimacy is created, hiding the source of the funds.

Reselling purchased antiques or artwork is a common step in the laundering process, creating the appearance of legal business dealings. To conduct these sales, criminals might employ middlemen or front companies, further obscuring the money trail. Reselling works of art through legitimate channels, like reputable auction houses or private galleries, lends the transactions more credibility.

The lack of transparency in the art market is one of the clear benefits of using transactions involving fine art and antiques for money laundering. Confidentiality, little regulation, and some subjectivity in valuations are characteristics of the market. These elements make it difficult for authorities to check transactions, identify owners, and spot irregularities.

Additionally, the frequent cross-border sales of antiques and works of art give criminals more opportunities to take advantage of jurisdictional complexities and make it more difficult to track down illicit funds. Criminals have opportunities to transfer money covertly across borders and continents thanks to the global nature of the art market.

SHELL COMPANIES

Shell companies, which have no assets or operations but appear to be legitimate businesses on paper, are a common tactic at this stage. Criminals create an additional layer of separation between themselves and the tainted money by routing funds through these entities. Offshore accounts, which are known for their confidentiality and lack of regulatory oversight, also play an important role.

These accounts allow the laundering process to cross national borders, complicating efforts to determine the true origin of the funds.

The consequences of concealing the source of illicit funds are far-reaching. It corrodes the integrity of financial systems, erodes public trust, and perpetuates a culture of impunity, in addition to assisting criminals in evading justice. Furthermore, it indirectly fuels a variety of criminal enterprises because the cleaned funds re-enter the criminal ecosystem, funding additional illegal activities.

A shell company, also known as a shell corporation or shell entity, is a type of business structure that exists only on paper but has few to no significant operational activities, assets, or legitimate business purpose. Instead of engaging in active business operations, a shell company frequently serves as a vehicle for various financial transactions, investments, or, in some cases, illicit activities.

These types of companies are frequently formed to achieve specific financial goals, such as tax evasion, asset protection, or confidentiality. They can be used for legal and legitimate purposes such as asset holding, mergers and acquisitions, and intellectual property management. However, because of their lack of transparency and oversight, they can be used for illegal activities such as money laundering, fraud, and the concealment of illicit funds.

Criminals may establish shell companies in the context of money laundering to create a seemingly legitimate front through which they can funnel their illegally obtained funds. Criminals attempt to obscure the source of the funds by conducting transactions through these shell entities, creating a complex web that makes it difficult for authorities to trace the money back to its criminal origin. Shell companies add another layer of separation between the criminal and the illicit funds, making it more difficult for law enforcement to connect the dots.

Shell companies can be formed in countries with lax regulations, making it easier to conceal ownership and financial activities. These jurisdictions are also known as "tax havens" or "offshore financial centers." Such locations provide a level of confidentiality that can be used by those looking to conduct financial transactions away from prying eyes and stringent regulations.

It is important to note that not all shell companies are illegal or involved in illegal activities. Many legitimate businesses use shell companies for legitimate purposes such as asset holding or complex financial transactions. However, because of the potential for abuse, governments, and regulatory bodies in several countries have put in place measures to increase transparency and prevent shell companies from being used for criminal purposes.

TERRORIST FINANCING TECHNIQUES

The channels mentioned, hereafter, provide a comprehensive overview of some of the techniques utilized to finance terrorists and acts of terrorism. However, it's important to note that these channels are not exhaustive, and there may exist additional methods and strategies employed by terrorist organizations to secure funds for their activities. The evolving nature of financial crimes necessitates ongoing vigilance and adaptation to address and prevent terrorist financing in all its forms effectively.

CLASSICAL CHANNELS

Terrorist organisations use a variety of methods to fund their operations, often utilizing classical financing channels that are easily accessible and appear to be inconspicuous. One popular method is to use legitimate financial systems to transfer funds across borders and conceal their origins. This may include wire transfers, electronic transactions, or the use of intermediaries to transfer funds between accounts in different countries.

The complexity of these transactions can make it difficult for authorities to trace the flow of funds back to their source.

CHARITIES AND NON-PROFIT ORGANISATIONS

Terrorists also use charities and non-profit organisations as fronts for raising and funneling funds. By posing as legitimate humanitarian or religious organisations, these groups can attract donations from unsuspecting individuals who believe their contributions are going to legitimate causes.

However, the funds are frequently diverted to fund terrorist activities, with only a small portion going towards the stated charitable purposes. This tactic takes advantage of people's willingness to help those in need, making it difficult to distinguish between genuine charities and those supporting illicit agendas.

EXTORTION AND KIDNAPPING FOR RANSOM

Terrorist groups frequently use extortion and kidnapping for ransom to secure funds. Extortion is the coercion of individuals, businesses, or even governments to make payments under threat of violence or damage. Kidnapping for ransom also targets individuals, and the ransom is typically demanded in exchange for their safe release. These tactics not only generate funds directly but also create an atmosphere of fear, which can help terrorists achieve their goals. In some cases, ransom payments can be substantial, providing groups with a significant source of income to sustain their operations.

INFORMAL FINANCIAL SYSTEMS

In addition to the traditional channels mentioned earlier, terrorist organizations often resort to informal financial systems to facilitate their funding needs. These methods operate outside the boundaries of formal banking systems and regulatory oversight. Some key examples include:

- Hawala and Informal Money Transfer Systems: Hawala is a centuries-old informal money transfer method prevalent in many regions around the world.

It involves a network of individuals who act as brokers, facilitating cross-border transfers without the need for physical movement of funds. Despite its legitimate uses, terrorist groups exploit hawala networks to move money discreetly and evade detection.

- Use of Cash Couriers and Smuggling: Cash couriers

are individuals who physically carry large amounts of money across borders. Terrorist organizations may recruit individuals or use sympathizers to transport funds to intended recipients or safe locations. This method allows them to bypass electronic transaction traces and monetary restrictions.

THE USE OF CYBER CHANNELS

Terrorist organisations have begun to utilize the virtual realm of cyberspace as a means of capitalizing on the monetary benefits of technological advancements in this age of information. These digital strategies open up new avenues for financial support and make it possible for organisations to communicate with people all over the world while retaining some measure of privacy. The following are some notable methods:

They take advantage of the power of the internet to raise money from sympathizers all over the world by engaging in online fundraising and crowdsourcing. They create campaigns by utilizing social media platforms, online forums, and websites in order to appeal to the ideologies of their supporters. They raise funds for a variety of activities, such as recruitment, the dissemination of propaganda, and operational expenses, through these campaigns.

For illustration purposes, a made-up terrorist organisation launches an online crowdfunding campaign with the goal of raising money to pay for the training of new recruits. They make an appeal to those who sympathize with them by emphasizing the significance of their cause and the necessity of monetary support to enable them to carry out their activities.

The Utilization of Cryptocurrencies for the Purpose of Anonymity Cryptocurrencies, such as Bitcoin, offer a level of anonymity that cannot be provided by traditional financial systems. Terrorist organisations make use of this function so that they can receive and transfer funds without leaving a trace of their activities in written form. They can avoid detection and circumvent financial institutions thanks to cryptocurrencies' decentralized nature. As an illustration, a made-up terrorist organisation accepts financial support in the form of cryptocurrency donations via a digital wallet. They use sophisticated methods of mixing funds to conceal where the money came from, making it more difficult for law enforcement to connect the money they launder to the illegal activities in which they engage.

Now that we've unpacked the key terms and sneaky tricks used in money laundering and terrorism financing, let's switch gears and dive into the red flags or 'warning signs' that can tip you off when dealing with shady characters.

THE RED FLAGS

A red flag is a warning sign or an indication that something might be wrong or suspicious. It's like a signal that alerts us to pay attention and be cautious. Red flags can be behaviours, actions, or circumstances that raise concerns and suggest that there may be a problem, or a potential risk involved.

Here are some signs you may come across when interacting with people. But! It's important to remember that noticing these signs doesn't automatically mean the person is doing something wrong. They only serve as a reminder to be more cautious when dealing with such individuals. I strongly recommend talking to your parents or trusted adults about your observations for guidance and support.

The examples I've mentioned below are just a few, and there may be more. I specifically focused on "friends" because I know you may see your friends as closer to you than your family during your teenage years. Unfortunately, this closeness can make it easier for deception to occur if you choose the wrong friends. It's essential to be aware of this and be cautious when forming relationships and friendships:

- Unexplained Wealth: Your friend suddenly starts buying expensive gadgets and designer clothes and going on lavish vacations, despite needing a clear source of income.

- Dishonesty or Lack of Transparency: Your friend frequently lies about their financial situation, claiming to have a part-time job while receiving large sums of money from unknown sources.

- Financial Struggles: Your friend seems to be struggling to make ends meet, yet always has access to large amounts of cash or expensive items, which they need help explaining.

- Unusual Financial Activities: You notice your friend making frequent large cash withdrawals and deposits without reasonable explanation or engaging in suspicious online transactions.

- Unwillingness to Cooperate: Your friend becomes defensive and evasive whenever you ask about their financial activities or involvement in certain transactions.

- Engaging in High-Risk Activities: Your friend convinces you to invest in a scheme that promises unbelievably high returns within a short period without providing concrete details or guarantees.

- Lack of Empathy or Moral Compass: Your friend shows little concern for the financial consequences of their actions, often disregarding the impact it may have on others or engaging in scams that exploit vulnerable individuals.

- Association with Known Criminals: You observe your friend regularly spending time with individuals involved in financial crimes or with a reputation for fraudulent activities.

If you find the amount of information overwhelming and worry about remembering every single flag, here are a couple of helpful tips for spotting potential issues:

- Red Flags often involve unusual and abnormal behaviours, circumstances, or requests.

- Red flags usually indicate something unusual or abnormal and tend to repeat themselves, showing up consistently.

Remember, identifying a red flag doesn't automatically mean the other person is suspicious. It's more of a caution sign that suggests you should be careful and not overlook potential concerns just for the sake of maintaining a friendly relationship.

SECTION THREE:
THE IMPACT

T he intricate web of financial crimes has a significant economic impact, which is the focus of this chapter. Beyond the immediate victims, the effects of these illegal activities spread throughout economies, sectors, and countries, leaving a permanent stain on stability and prosperity. We will investigate the complex relationships between financial crimes and economic disruption, revealing the mechanisms by which illegal financial activity undermines the very basis of financial stability.

This Section illuminates the extensive economic consequences of financial crimes, ranging from declining investor confidence to distortion of market dynamics. We will explore the cascading effects of money laundering, fraud, and corruption through case studies and real-world examples, showing how these actions reverberate throughout history and affect various industries.

CHAPTER SEVEN: THE ECONOMIC IMPLICATIONS

Understanding the impact of financial crimes is crucial in a world where their reach extends far and wide. These crimes go beyond harming individuals or corporations; they strike at the core of our economic fabric causing ripple effects that can be felt across entire countries. The significance of this issue goes beyond monetary loss; it puts at risk the integrity, stability, and growth of economies.

In this chapter we will thoroughly examine the ways in which financial crimes impact the economic landscape. The consequences range from distorting market competition to eroding trust in financial institutions. We will delve into some of the severe and far-reaching outcomes shedding light on how these crimes can hinder innovation, undermine social welfare and create unseen barriers to economic progress.

The following pages do not unveil the hidden side of financial wrongdoing only, but also aim to equip readers, particularly our younger generation, with the knowledge necessary to recognize and combat these dangerous threats.

These are not theoretical ideas; they have genuine and tangible consequences that affect people's lives, businesses, and entire societies. Get ready for an exploration into the mysterious realm of financial misconduct and its lasting effects on our economic health.

ECONOMIC DISRUPTION: FINANCIAL CRIMES' WIDE-REACHING EFFECTS

Financial crimes have a significant and pervasive impact on economies all over the world, causing economic disruption that ripples through different societal sectors and strata. The intricate ways that illegal activity sneaks in and undermines the very foundations of economic systems are what causes this disruption.

The loss of faith in financial markets and institutions is one of the most obvious effects of financial crimes. The efficient operation of markets is jeopardized when people and companies hesitate to transact because they are worried about fraud, money laundering, and insider trading. This loss of trust hinders economic growth, discourages investment, and fosters an atmosphere of uncertainty.

Financial crimes disturb the equilibrium of supply and demand in markets. Stock price manipulation, dishonest trading methods, and market rigging alter market dynamics, causing incorrect resource allocation and unfair competition. This disruption has the potential to significantly impact many different industries and ways of life by causing asset bubbles, market crashes, and economic downturns.

Financial crimes also take resources away from worthwhile and legal endeavours. The money that is stolen through fraud, bribery, and illegal financial transfers could have been invested in science, infrastructure, and the growth of human capital. This resource misallocation impedes economic development and prolongs underdevelopment cycles.

LACK OF TRUST: HOW FINANCIAL CRIMES HURT INVESTOR CONFIDENCE.

In the world of finance, transactions and investments can't happen without trust. But the effects of financial crimes are far-reaching and hurt more than just the people who are directly affected. They also hurt investor confidence. Fraud, insider trading, and other illegal financial activities hurt people's trust in each other. This has far-reaching effects that go beyond individual incidents.

Investor confidence is a fine line that depends on openness, fairness, and doing the right thing. Financial crimes upset this balance because they make it harder to believe that financial markets are fair. When investors think that markets are being manipulated, that insider information is being used against them, or that fraud could happen to their investments, they are less likely to invest.

One of the most important effects of a trust deficit is less money coming in. Investors become careful and hesitant because they are afraid that their hard-earned money could be manipulated or stolen. This decreased willingness to invest means that there is less money available for businesses and projects, which slows down economic growth and innovation. Also, it makes it harder for emerging markets to get foreign investments, which keeps the cycle of underdevelopment going.

Financial crimes also contribute to market instability. When sudden and unexpected evidence of fraud comes to light, it can cause panic selling, which sends stock prices tumbling.

This instability hurts individual investors and also hurts the stability of the financial markets as a whole. As investors' confidence drops, the market's behaviour becomes more volatile, which makes it hard for them to make good decisions.

The loss of trust hurts financial institutions in many ways. When scandals about wrongdoing in the financial world come to light, it's hard for institutions to fix the damage to their reputations.

Customers can take out their deposits, and regulators can fine the institution, which puts even more pressure on its finances. Also, a lack of trust in one institution can spread to other companies in the same industry, which hurts the reputation of the whole financial sector.

MARKET MANIPULATION: DISTORTED DYNAMICS CAUSED BY ILLICIT ACTIVITIES.

The goal of financial markets is to be efficient, reflecting the knowledge and wisdom of investors as a whole. But the effects of financial crimes, especially market manipulation, can change these dynamics and make a place where unfairness and uncertainty can grow.

Market manipulation includes a wide range of sneaky ways to change prices on the market, which goes against the basic rules of supply and demand.

One way to manipulate the market is to make a security or asset seem more valuable than it really is in order to attract investors and drive-up prices.

Criminals may spread false information or rumors to make it seem like there is more demand, which may lead investors who don't know what's going to buy. As the prices go up, these criminals sell their investments and make a lot of money before the bubble bursts and prices go down, hurting other investors.

On the other hand, thieves may do "bear raids," in which they try to drive down the prices of assets. This strategy involves selling a lot of assets, which causes investors to panic and drives prices down. Once the prices have dropped enough, the criminals buy the assets back at lower prices, making more money at the expense of others.

Not only does market manipulation hurt individual investors, but it also hurts the markets as a whole. It destroys the idea that prices are based on real supply and demand, which makes investors question how far the system is.

This loss of trust can make people less likely to join and more likely to look for other ways to invest their money.

Also, market manipulation can affect the whole system. Price distortions can have a domino effect on related industries, institutions, and even economies.

It can lead to a waste of resources, which hurts economic growth and stability. Market manipulation doesn't just lead to financial losses; it has broader effects on the economy.

Let me explain in a more simple way and start from top:

What's Market Manipulation, Anyway?

Imagine the stock market as a big, buzzing marketplace where everyone's shouting, buying, and selling stuff. Normally, prices go up and down based on how many people want something and how much of it there is—this is "supply and demand," the backbone of any market.

Sneaky Moves to Game the System

1. Pump and Dump:

- What's Weird: Someone's hyping up a stock like it's the next big thing, using social media or even insider tips.

- Why It's Bad: People buy the stock, thinking it's going to make them rich. But then, the hype-man sells his shares, the price tanks, and you're left holding worthless stock.

2. Bear Raids:

- What's Weird: Suddenly, a stock's price starts to nosedive.

- Why It's Bad: Some people are selling a bunch of shares to freak everyone else out. As the price drops, they buy it back cheap.

Why It's More Than Just Losing Money?

1. Trust Goes Down the Drain:

Market manipulation makes people lose trust in the financial markets. And if people can't trust it, why would they invest their money in it?

2. Domino Effect:

Messing with one stock's price can affect the prices of related companies. It can even cause problems for the economy as a whole.

3. Resource Waste:

Imagine all the energy and time you put into researching and investing, only for it to be a lie. That's a lot of wasted resources, which hurts the economy's overall health.

The Bigger Picture

When trust is lost, everyone loses. This can make people abandon the financial markets and look for other places to put their money, like under their mattresses (okay, maybe not literally, but you get the point). And when that happens, the whole system suffers, from the smallest investors to the big corporations.

So, in a way, market manipulation isn't just stealing money; it's stealing the fairness, trust, and stability that an economy needs to be healthy. It's a big deal, and that's why it's so important to understand what it is and how to spot it.

DRAINING PUBLIC COFFERS: THE TOLL OF FINANCIAL CRIMES ON GOVERNMENT FINANCES

Financial crimes have a long-lasting effect on government finances because they steal money from the public purse and give it to criminals. The effects go beyond the people who were hurt and the businesses that were hurt. They also affect society by reducing public services, raising taxes, and making people less trusting of government institutions.

Tax evasion is one way that financial crimes hurt the government's finances in a big way. When people, businesses, or even criminal groups use scams to avoid paying taxes, the government loses a large amount of money that it could have used to pay for important services and infrastructure projects. This lack of money makes it harder for governments to provide education, health care, social services, and other important things that are important for the well-being of society.

Also, the money from financial crimes may be "washed" through complicated schemes, making it hard for the government to find and get back. This hidden money is taken out of circulation, which makes things even worse for government budgets. As financial criminals try to avoid paying taxes, governments have to raise taxes on law-abiding citizens to make up for the shortfall. This leads to an unfair distribution of the tax burden.

Another effect of financial crimes is that the government has to spend more time and money on investigating, prosecuting, and enforcing the law. These activities not only take a lot of time and money, but they also keep people from working on other important problems. Law enforcement agencies must spend a lot of money to fight financial crimes. If they didn't, they could use those funds to stop other kinds of crime or meet societal needs.

Also, when people lose faith in government institutions because of financial crimes, it can make it harder to collect taxes. People may lose faith in the government's ability to run a fair and just financial system, which could make them less likely to follow tax laws and other financial rules.

RESOURCE DRAIN: HOW ILLICIT WEALTH DEPLETES NATIONAL RESOURCES

The effects of financial crimes reach far beyond the people who are directly affected and the financial institutions they work for. They also affect the core of national economies. The flow of illegal money out of a country causes a resource drain, which is one of the most serious effects. This drain causes serious economic problems and slows down sustainable development.

Illegal financial flows, which are caused by financial crimes like money laundering and corruption, take money away from public services, infrastructure projects, and social programs that are more important. This loss of capital hurts the economic growth of a country and makes it harder for people from different backgrounds to get ahead. One part of this loss of resources is capital flight, which is when people and businesses move their money abroad to avoid taxes, get around rules, or protect money they got illegally.

This not only decreases the amount of money that can be invested in a country, but it also reduces the amount of tax money that could be used to pay for public goods. Also, financial crimes can make it harder for skilled professionals and entrepreneurs to find work in their home countries. This is because corruption, a lack of economic transparency, and a lack of access to justice make it hard for them to do so. This loss of human capital makes it harder for a country to come up with new ideas, compete globally, and build a sustainable economy based on knowledge.

Also, the illegal flow of money can keep poverty and inequality from getting better. When money meant for development is put into offshore accounts or used to buy luxury goods in other countries, it wastes the chance to help poor communities and invest in education, health care, and social services.

FLIGHT OF CAPITAL: INVESTOR AVERSION DUE TO FINANCIAL CRIMES

Financial crimes cast a long shadow over the world of investing. They create constant uncertainty and make investors less sure that financial systems are honest. The "flight of capital" describes the movement of money out of a country or region because people are worried about financial crimes, corruption, and a lack of openness.

In the wake of financial scandals, fraud, and money laundering, investors often have to rethink their risk assessments and allocation strategies. This cautious approach can make people less likely to invest in foreign direct investment (FDI), leave domestic markets, and take part in long-term economic activities. The flight of capital shows up in many ways, such as when foreign investors leave, when local investors don't want to invest in their own economies, and when foreign aid and grants go down. As investors look for safer and more stable markets, it may become harder for countries with much financial crime to attract the capital they need for economic growth and development. There are many effects of capital leaving a country. With less investment, it will be harder to create jobs, build infrastructure, and encourage new ideas. This can slow down economic growth, make unemployment rates go up, and make income inequality worse.

Also, when money leaves a country, it can put a strain on government budgets, leaving less money for public services and social programs. Bringing back investor confidence and stopping money from leaving the country will take more than one thing. Strengthening financial regulations, making them clearer, and going after financial criminals in a fair way send a clear message that illegal activities won't be accepted.

A comprehensive anti-money laundering and counter-terrorism financing frameworks, along with strong enforcement, help to reassure investors that the financial system is being closely watched and regulated.

CHAPTER EIGHT: THE PSYCHOLOGICAL IMPLICATIONS

This chapter delves into an often-overlooked aspect of the aftermath of financial crimes: the profound psychological impact they leave in their wake. While the tangible consequences of financial crimes are evident, such as economic losses and legal repercussions, the emotional toll on individuals, families, and communities is equally significant. This chapter sheds light on the intricate ways in which financial crimes reverberate within the human psyche, leaving behind scars that may be invisible but are deeply felt.

TRUST EROSION AND DISTRUST

Financial crimes often strike at the heart of trust, both on a personal and institutional level. Victims who fall prey to scams or fraud committed by individuals they trusted may experience a profound sense of betrayal. This can lead to skepticism and wariness, not only toward individuals but also toward financial institutions and systems. The breach of trust can cast a long shadow, making it difficult for victims to rebuild relationships or have faith in financial processes.

EMOTIONAL DISTRESS

The emotional toll of financial crimes is not limited to financial losses alone. Victims can experience a range of intense emotions, from anger and frustration to anxiety and sadness. The sudden realization that their hard-earned money has been stolen or misused can trigger feelings of shock and disbelief. As victims navigate legal processes to recover their assets, emotional distress can intensify, leading to sleep disturbances, mood swings, and a general decline in mental well-being.

IMPACT ON MENTAL HEALTH

The stress and uncertainty resulting from financial crimes can have serious implications for mental health. Victims may experience symptoms of depression, anxiety, and heightened levels of stress. The fear of financial instability, coupled with the burden of dealing with legal procedures, can take a toll on mental and emotional resilience. Elderly victims, who may have invested a lifetime of savings, can experience an additional layer of emotional distress due to the fear of financial ruin during their later years.

SOCIAL ISOLATION

The shame and embarrassment associated with being a victim of financial crimes can lead to social isolation. Victims may withdraw from their social circles, fearing judgment or pity from others. The stigma attached to falling victim to fraud or scams can create feelings of humiliation, making it difficult for individuals to share their experiences with friends or family.

CYNICISM AND MISTRUST

Witnessing or experiencing financial crimes can breed a sense of cynicism and mistrust in interpersonal relationships. Victims may find it challenging to believe the intentions of others, leading to strained interactions. This mistrust can extend beyond financial matters, affecting personal relationships and professional collaborations.

COLLECTIVE IMPACT

The repercussions of financial crimes are not confined to individual victims alone. When corruption and financial wrongdoing become prevalent in a society, they can erode ethical standards and create a culture of dishonesty. This collective impact can lead to a breakdown in social cohesion and the erosion of values that underpin a functioning society.

CHAPTER NINE: THE SOCIAL AND CULTURAL IMPLICATIONS

As we gain more knowledge about crimes committed against financial institutions, it is becoming increasingly apparent that these crimes have effects that extend beyond simple monetary losses. In this chapter, we pull back the curtain to reveal the intricate ways in which financial crimes shape our societies and put our cultural norms to the test. These effects have far-reaching effects that reverberate throughout social and cultural landscapes. Some examples of these effects include a decrease in trust and a widening of wealth gaps.

A REDUCTION IN TRUST AND AN INCREASE IN SKEPTICISM

Because financial crimes strike at the very core of trust, they cause us to have skepticism both towards financial institutions and towards other people. The more people hear about cons, frauds, and thefts of money, the more skeptical they become regarding business transactions involving money. This breach of trust can affect more than just one's financial situation and can lead to skepticism about many different aspects of life. When people stop trusting one another, the social fabric becomes frayed, and relationships become strained.

WIDENING THE WEALTH GAP

People who are already having a difficult time making ends meet often have to pay for the dirty money that these crimes bring in. Those who are suffering the most are the ones who bear the brunt of injustice and inequality, which contributes to an increasingly tense society. The anger that inevitably follows can be a source of trouble for society.

EFFECTS ON CULTURAL VALUES

Cultural values are what bind a society together and guide how people behave and interact with each other. They are also what contribute to a sense of identity for individuals within that society. The pursuit of personal gain at the expense of the good of the group is at odds with these values and can constitute a basis for financial crimes.

People may find it more difficult to care about things like cooperation, shared responsibility, and empathy as the culture shifts towards a greater emphasis on materialism and self-interest.

THE STIGMA AND SHAME ASSOCIATED WITH IT

Some victims might experience feelings of shame, embarrassment, and anger directed towards themselves. This emotional burden can cause people to withdraw from other people out of fear of what their friends and family will think of them.

This fear can cause people to isolate themselves. People who have been duped by fraud or scams may be reluctant to discuss their experiences openly, which makes it more difficult for them to receive assistance when they need it.

THE WAY THE MEDIA REPORT ON HIGH-PROFILE FINANCIAL CRIMES AFFECTS THE WAY PEOPLE THINK

It's possible that people will have less trust in financial transactions when things of this nature occur more frequently. This can have the effect of putting a damper on legitimate economic activities, which in turn makes people less likely to try to make money and slows down economic growth.

IMPLEMENTING MORE STRINGENT RULES AND INCREASING THE AMOUNT OF OVERSIGHT

Although taking these measures is essential to reducing the number of crimes committed, they have the potential to make people anxious and suspicious. It's possible that the sheer volume of regulations will give people the impression that the financial system is fraught with danger, which could stifle economic innovation.

CHAPTER TEN: THE GLOBAL IMPACT

As we delve into the world of financial crimes, it becomes evident that their impact extends far beyond individual victims and local communities. In the interconnected fabric of our global society, the consequences of financial crimes reverberate across borders, affecting economies, governments, and individuals on an international scale. Beyond economic repercussions, financial crimes pose a significant threat to global security.

This couple of pages Chpater unravels, in a nutshell, the intricate web of global consequences wrought by these illicit activities. Here are some of the implications expected:

Funding Terrorism:

Financial crimes like money laundering can give terrorists the money they need to carry out attacks. Think about it like this: Imagine a group wants to blow up a bridge in another country. They'll need money to buy materials and maybe even to pay people who are helping them. If someone funnels money to them through financial crimes, they're essentially giving them the tools to go through with their dangerous plans.

Empowering Organized Crime:

When people commit financial crimes, they can give money to groups that do bad stuff like sell drugs or weapons. This makes these groups stronger and more dangerous. Imagine if a street gang suddenly had lots of cash—they could buy better weapons, recruit more members, and extend their "business" to other countries.

Corruption and Governance:

Let's say a politician in one country takes a bribe from a big company to do them a favor. Now, that politician owes something to that company, which messes up how decisions are made. This could affect relationships with other countries and make people lose trust in their leaders.

Economic Instability:

Picture this: A huge bank is tricked into giving out loans that people can't pay back. Eventually, the bank crashes, and it's such a big deal that it impacts other countries' economies too. People lose jobs, and when people are struggling to make ends meet, they're less happy and more likely to protest or even riot.

Diverting Resources:

If a country is busy spending all its money to stop financial crimes, it can't spend money on other things that matter, like schools or hospitals. This affects not just one country but also its neighbors. For example, if one country can't afford to maintain a good healthcare system, a disease outbreak could spread to nearby countries.

Information Warfare:

Imagine if someone used money earned from financial crimes to spread lies on the internet about another country's leader. People could start to believe those lies, and it might lead to disagreements or conflicts between countries.

Trade Implications:

If someone uses illegal money to buy a ton of stuff from another country, it could mess up how much things are supposed to cost. This can affect relationships between countries and could even lead to a trade war where countries stop buying and selling stuff from each other.

Normalizing Illicit Activities:

If people see that financial crimes are happening all the time and no one gets caught, they might think it's not a big deal to commit these crimes. This can make the problem even worse, and it sends a message to people in other countries that it's easy to get away with financial crimes.

Resource Wars:

Sometimes, the money from financial crimes ends up in places where people are fighting over resources like water or oil. This extra money can make those conflicts even worse and might even pull other countries into the conflict.

Global Network:

Nowadays, you can send money all over the world with just a click. While that's cool for many reasons, it's also easier for bad guys to move money between countries. This means that stopping these crimes isn't just one country's problem; everyone has to work together to solve it.

SECTION FOUR:
THE FIGHT

This is the fourth section of the book, "The Fight." At this critical stage, we shift from attempting to determine how bad financial crimes are to taking action against them.

Here, I will provide you with the knowledge and tools you need to not only react to suspected exploitation but also fight it back.

We will discuss the roles and jobs that are important in the fight against these crimes. This will provide you with a potential career path if you want to help this cause. In addition, we will demonstrate how the global community has banded together to combat financial crimes by examining how global organisations and task forces are collaborating to stop these illegal activities.

You'll not only have the tools to protect yourself and others from exploitation by the end of this section, but you'll also have a better understanding of the various roles, jobs, and collaborative projects that are paving the way for a safer financial landscape.

CHAPTER ELEVEN: THE RIGHT REACTION

It is imperative that a teenager takes proactive measures to protect themselves and others whenever they sense or suspect that they are the target of financial exploitation or a potential scam. Everyone, regardless of age, is a potential victim of financial exploitation; therefore, the ability to remain vigilant is an absolutely necessary skill to acquire.

The following is a comprehensive guide on what a teenager should do when they have a suspicion that they are the victim of a financial crime or exploitation:

REMAIN CALM AND TRUST YOUR INSTINCTS

Trusting your instincts is like having your internal radar system. If a situation triggers a feeling of discomfort, unease, or suspicion, it's crucial to acknowledge and honor that sensation. Your instincts are finely tuned to pick up on nuances that might not be immediately apparent. They act as an early warning system that something might be amiss. Remaining calm in such situations is essential. It prevents you from making impulsive decisions under pressure.

Imagine you receive a phone call from an unknown number claiming that you've won a prize, but they need your bank details to process it. If your gut feeling raises a red flag about the authenticity of the call, it's important not to let excitement or pressure cloud your judgment. Take a deep breath, remind yourself to stay calm, and avoid divulging any personal or financial information until you're absolutely sure of the caller's identity.

Trusting your instincts is about respecting your inner voice. It's not about succumbing to fear or paranoia but acknowledging that your intuition has a valuable role to play in keeping you safe.

So, whether you're faced with an unexpected offer, a strange message, or an unfamiliar situation, remember that your instincts are your allies. By staying composed and heeding those intuitive warnings, you're empowering yourself to navigate potential risks with wisdom and confidence.

CONFIRM THE SOURCE

Currently, there are many different ways to communicate, such as emails, text messages, and phone calls. Unfortunately, there are also many different ways for people to try to defraud you. Verifying the veracity of the origin of any communication that comes as a surprise or is out of the ordinary is one of the most important precautions you can take to safeguard yourself against being taken advantage of financially.

Imagine that you have received an email that purports to come from your bank and urges you to update the information associated with your account immediately. There is a possibility that the email is genuine, complete with logos and language that sounds official. Take a moment to compose yourself and proceed with extreme caution before clicking on any links contained within the email or directly responding to the sender.

The first step is to conduct an independent search for the official contact information of your bank by using a reliable source, such as the bank's official website or a recent bank statement. Instead of calling the bank using the contact information that was provided in the email, you should call the bank using the information that you found on your own.

This way, you will be able to determine whether the email really came from your bank or whether it was an attempt to steal your information.

Your Independent verification is your best defence against falling for phishing scams, in which con artists pose as reputable businesses in an effort to trick you into divulging sensitive personal information or financial data.

You can protect yourself from the possibility of being exploited financially if you take the additional precaution of verifying the origin of any unexpected communication that you receive.

Even if someone is trying to deceive you and manipulate you, you will still be able to take control of the situation and make decisions based on accurate information if you implement this straightforward but effective tactic.

Keep in mind that it is always preferable to err on the side of caution and conduct additional research rather than to rush into something that could result in monetary loss.

DO YOUR RESEARCH BEFORE MAKING ANY
FINANCIAL DECISIONS OR INVESTMENTS

In a world brimming with opportunities and information, it's crucial to approach financial decisions and investments with a healthy dose of skepticism and thorough research. The promise of quick gains or enticing deals might be tempting, but the path to sound financial choices begins with diligent investigation.

Picture this scenario: you stumble upon an investment opportunity that guarantees incredibly high returns within an unrealistically short timeframe. It seems like a dream come true, but as the age-old adage goes, "If it sounds too good to be true, it probably is." This is where your research skills become your armor against potential exploitation.

Start by delving into the details of the company, individual, or deal that's caught your attention. Utilize the vast resources available on the internet to your advantage. Please search for the company's official website, reviews from legitimate sources, and their presence on reputable online platforms. A credible company should have a professional website, a history of positive interactions, and a transparent presence within the online community.

However, the absence of a website or a scarcity of information should raise red flags. Financial decisions involve your hard-earned money, and any legitimate entity should have a digital footprint that verifies its authenticity.

Furthermore, educate yourself about common investment practices and financial norms. Understand the market trends, typical rates of return, and the potential risks associated with certain investment ventures. If an opportunity deviates drastically from these established norms, it's essential to exercise caution.

Remember, conducting research doesn't require you to be an expert; it's about being an informed and proactive decision-maker. By dedicating time to research and critically evaluating opportunities, you're taking an empowered step towards safeguarding your financial interests.

So, before you dive into any investment or financial commitment, take a breath, and embark on your detective journey – your financial future will thank you for it.

There are definitely ways that teens could be exploited financially without the knowledge of adults or parents. While formal investment platforms generally require participants to be 18 or older, the internet has opened up a Pandora's Box of potentially predatory or risky ventures that could be accessible to teens. Here are some examples:

- Virtual Goods and In-Game Items: Video game platforms sometimes allow trading or selling of in-game items. Teens could be led to believe that these digital assets are 'investments' and may spend large sums of real money.

- Social Media "Investment" Groups: Online communities could promise high returns on investments that require no adult supervision. Teens could be swayed into joining these groups and contributing money, not knowing the risks involved.

- Influencer-Promoted Schemes: Popular online personalities might promote 'get-rich-quick' schemes, exploiting their influence over a younger audience. They may advertise that these investments are tailored for their young viewers.

- Sketchy Online Courses: Websites might offer courses or 'investment secrets,' claiming that they are specially designed for young people to make money quickly. These could be scams that exploit a teen's lack of financial knowledge.

- Mobile Apps with In-App Purchases: Some apps are geared toward financial trading or investment simulations but offer in-app purchases that promise better returns or extra features. This could be a slippery slope for teens using their or their parents' credit cards.

- Pyramid Schemes and MLM for Teens: Teens could be recruited for these under the guise of 'entrepreneurial initiatives' targeted specifically at young people, saying things like, "You don't need adults to make money."

Red Flags:

- No clear way to cash out or receive returns

- Promises of high returns with no risk

- Pressure to act quickly

- Requests for personal or financial information

- Any sort of 'membership fee' or upfront payment

Many of these scenarios could fall into a gray area, especially if there's no explicit law against the activity. However, they are often highly unethical and exploitative.

REFRAIN FROM SHARING PERSONAL INFORMATION

In the digital age, where information flows freely and connections are just a click away, the importance of guarding your personal information cannot be overstated.

Your sensitive data, such as your social security number, bank details, and passwords, are like keys to your financial kingdom. Protecting these keys is paramount to preventing potential financial exploitation.

Imagine receiving a message or a call from someone who

claims to represent a reputable organization or institution. They request your personal information under the pretext of verifying your identity or offering you an exciting opportunity.

While it may appear innocuous, handing over your personal information without due diligence can have far-reaching consequences.

Con artists and scammers are skilled at manipulation. They know how to gain your trust, and once they have access to your personal information, they can wreak havoc on your financial life.

Identity theft is a grave concern, where criminals use stolen data to commit fraud, open new accounts, or even access your existing financial accounts.

LOOK FOR WARNING SIGNS

In the world of financial transactions, vigilance is your best ally. Scammers and fraudsters are adept at crafting convincing narratives that often mask their true intentions. To shield yourself from falling into their traps, it's essential to be aware of common warning signs that indicate a potential scam or con. In previous chapters, I have discussed several red flags and warning signs.

Notice the Warning Signs at Your Fingertips

The following list aims to simplify the identification of some signs, you might notice as a teenager, for ease of recognition:

Urgent Demands for Money

One telltale sign of a potential scam is the urgency with which the other party demands money or action from you. Scammers often create a sense of impending doom or urgency, pressuring you to act quickly without providing adequate time for you to think critically. Be cautious when someone insists that immediate financial action is the only solution to a supposed problem.

High-Pressure Tactics

Scammers thrive on creating pressure to make you act hastily. They might promise you an exclusive deal that's only available for a limited time or use fear tactics to make you believe that you're missing out on a vital opportunity.

If you feel like you're being pushed into making a decision without the opportunity to gather information or think it through, it's a red flag.

Promises of Guaranteed Profits

Be cautious of any situation that guarantees you guaranteed profits or returns that seem too good to be true. While everyone dreams of lucrative opportunities, legitimate investments come with inherent risks. If someone is promising you sky-high profits with no risk, it's likely a fraudulent scheme.

Requests for Payments in Advance

A classic move by scammers is to request an upfront payment for a service or product that hasn't materialized yet. They might claim it's a processing fee, a security deposit, or an administrative cost. However, legitimate businesses usually don't ask for upfront payments without delivering their end of the bargain first.

It's important to remember that awareness is your first line of defense. By becoming familiar with these warning signs, you'll be better equipped to recognize potentially fraudulent situations. If any of these signs appear in a transaction, communication, or proposal, take a step back and critically evaluate the situation.

Legitimate and reputable entities will always allow you time to make informed decisions. They won't pressure you into immediate actions, and they'll provide transparent information about risks and potential outcomes. If something seems off, trust your instincts, and take the time to research, verify, and seek advice from trusted sources before proceeding. Remember, the power to protect yourself from exploitation lies in your ability to spot these warning signs and respond with caution and confidence.

ASK TRUSTED ADULTS FOR ADVICE

In the maze of financial interactions, asking trusted adults for advice can be a source of clarity and knowledge. Never be afraid to reach out to the people in your life who have your best interests at heart if you ever find yourself involved in a circumstance that causes you to have questions or worries.

Your parents or guardians are the cornerstone of your support network. They have a wealth of life experience and wisdom that can guide you through challenging or intricate financial situations. Ask them the questions and voice your worries. Their advice can be very helpful in clarifying the situation and assisting you in making decisions. Teachers and school counsellors are important allies when it comes to learning practical life lessons in addition to being sources of academic knowledge. They are skilled at helping students who are dealing with a variety of difficulties by providing guidance and encouragement. These experts can provide viewpoints that you might not have thought of if you run into a financial situation that leaves you uneasy.

Consulting with dependable adults when facing financial uncertainties is crucial for a number of reasons. First and foremost, you may gain insights from their experience and viewpoint that you otherwise might not have. They can aid in your objective analysis of the situation while taking possible risks and advantages into account.

As teenagers, you are still figuring out the world's complexities, including its financial system. A different point of view from a reliable adult can help you comprehend the bigger picture and the effects of your choices. They may be able to effectively guide you because they have dealt with situations similar to yours in the past or because they can. You can take informed action by talking to reliable adults. They can assist you in weighing the advantages and disadvantages, determining the validity of offers, and assisting you in making decisions that are in your best interests. By following their advice, you can avoid falling victim to the pressure or emotional appeals that con artists frequently use.

How to Communicate With Your Trusted Circles?

When requesting advice, speak openly and honestly with respected adults. Share the specifics of the circumstance, your worries, and any information you have gathered. Even if their suggestions and opinions differ from your initial ones, be open to hearing them out. Keep in mind that their advice serves to empower you and safeguard you from harm. The assistance of dependable adults can serve as your anchor in a world where financial transactions occasionally can be confusing and complex. Along with providing wisdom, they also give you comfort in knowing that you're not travelling alone. So, whenever you find yourself in an uncertain situation, don't be afraid to ask for their advice. It's a sensible and responsible move that will protect your overall security and financial stability.

REPORT THE SUSPICIOUS ACTIVITY

If you come across something that appears to be a scam or a financial crime, you should report it to the appropriate authorities. You may wish to get in touch with the agency responsible for law enforcement in your area, the Federal Trade Commission (FTC), or one of the many other consumer protection agencies. By reporting suspicious activity, you can help protect other people from falling for the same cons.

Always remember to:

- Educate Yourself: Make sure you are up to date on the most recent types of cons and frauds. There are many organisations that offer resources and advice to help you maintain your vigilance. Your knowledge is your best weapon in the fight against exploitation.

- Take precautions with what information you share on

social media and other online platforms to safeguard your online reputation. Scammers can more effectively target you by using personal information they have obtained.

- Maintain an up-to-date version of your privacy settings and be wary of friend or connection requests coming from accounts you are not familiar with.

- Only Rely on Reliable Sources If you are considering making a financial decision or investment, you should only rely on reliable sources for information. It is in your best interest to seek the guidance of professionals, organisations, or certified financial advisors who have a solid reputation.

- And keep in mind that anyone can become a victim of financial exploitation; however, you can protect yourself and others from falling prey to scams and frauds by maintaining awareness, remaining vigilant, and taking the appropriate actions. Investing time and effort into developing these skills when you're young will serve you well throughout your entire life.

CHAPTER TWELVE: THE ROLES AND JOBS

In the relentless battle against financial crimes, an army of dedicated professionals stands ready to defend our economic landscape.

This chapter is a roadmap for those who wish to venture into the world of countering financial crimes, outlining a variety of roles and jobs that contribute to this critical endeavor. From cybersecurity experts to financial investigators, each role plays a unique part in upholding the integrity of financial systems and safeguarding individuals, businesses, and governments from the clutches of exploitation.

FINANCIAL INVESTIGATOR: UNCOVERING HIDDEN TRUTHS

Financial investigators are like modern-day detectives who use their financial acumen to unravel complex webs of deceit. They analyze financial records, transactions, and patterns to identify irregularities and suspicious activities. Working with law enforcement agencies, they gather evidence that can lead to the prosecution of those engaged in financial crimes.

These investigators often collaborate with law enforcement agencies, regulatory bodies, and private organizations to track illicit financial activities. Their analytical skills are crucial in untangling intricate money trails and piecing together evidence that can stand up in court. They may specialize in areas such as fraud, money laundering, or asset tracing. They work closely with legal teams to ensure that the evidence they gather is admissible in court.

CYBERSECURITY EXPERT: GUARDIAN OF DIGITAL FORTRESSES

Cybersecurity experts are the digital guardians who protect sensitive information and financial systems from cyberattacks. They design, implement, and maintain security measures to safeguard against data breaches, hacking, and online fraud.

In the digital age, financial transactions are increasingly conducted online. Cybersecurity experts work tirelessly to create robust defenses against cyber threats. They implement encryption, firewalls, and intrusion detection systems to shield financial institutions and individuals from cybercriminals seeking to exploit vulnerabilities. They stay updated on the latest cyber threats and constantly adapt their strategies to stay one step ahead of cybercriminals.

COMPLIANCE OFFICER: UPHOLDING ETHICAL STANDARDS

Compliance officers ensure that individuals and organizations adhere to regulatory and legal standards. In the realm of financial crimes, they play a vital role in preventing money laundering, fraud, and other illicit activities.

These professionals monitor and assess financial transactions, internal policies, and external regulations. They implement measures to prevent financial crimes and ensure that their organizations are in full compliance with relevant laws. Compliance officers collaborate closely with legal teams to navigate the intricate landscape of financial regulations. They also conduct internal audits to identify potential vulnerabilities and gaps in compliance.

FORENSIC ACCOUNTANT: PIECING TOGETHER THE PUZZLE

Forensic accountants are financial detectives who investigate financial discrepancies and anomalies. They meticulously analyze financial records to reconstruct events, uncover fraud, and present evidence in legal proceedings.

Forensic accountants are adept at sifting through financial data to identify inconsistencies or signs of manipulation. They may work in tandem with law enforcement agencies, attorneys, and corporate entities to support investigations and litigation related to financial crimes. They use advanced accounting techniques to trace money flows, identify fraudulent transactions, and quantify financial losses. Their findings are often used as crucial evidence in legal cases.

DATA ANALYST: EXTRACTING INSIGHTS
FROM INFORMATION

Data analysts leverage technology to extract meaningful insights from vast amounts of financial data. They identify patterns, trends, and anomalies that could indicate potential financial crimes.

Financial data is abundant and complex. Data analysts use specialized tools to process, analyze, and visualize data, helping organizations detect unusual patterns or activities: their insights guide decision-making and the implementation of risk mitigation strategies.

Data analysts collaborate with other professionals, such as investigators and compliance officers, to translate data insights into actionable strategies for preventing financial crimes.

ANTI-MONEY LAUNDERING SPECIALIST:
HALTING ILLICIT FLOWS

Anti-money laundering (AML) specialists are at the forefront of preventing money laundering and illicit financial activities. They develop and implement strategies to detect and report suspicious transactions.

AML specialists collaborate with financial institutions to establish protocols that identify and flag transactions that may be connected to money laundering. They analyze transaction data and report potential cases to relevant authorities. In short, They play a critical role in disrupting the financial flows that support criminal enterprises. And they constantly stay updated on evolving money laundering techniques and are trained to recognize patterns and behaviors associated with illicit financial activities.

LEGAL CONSULTANT: NAVIGATING LEGAL WATERS

Legal consultants provide guidance on the legal aspects of financial crimes. They ensure that individuals and organizations operate within the boundaries of relevant laws and regulations. They are well-versed in the intricate legal landscape surrounding financial crimes. And they provide advice on compliance, risk management, and litigation strategies.

Their expertise helps organizations navigate legal complexities and avoid legal pitfalls. They also work closely with compliance officers and investigators to ensure that all actions taken are legally sound and that investigations are conducted within the bounds of the law.

FINANCIAL EDUCATOR: EMPOWERING AWARENESS

Financial educators are advocates for financial literacy and awareness. They educate individuals about the risks of financial crimes and equip them with the knowledge needed to protect themselves.

Financial educators design and deliver workshops, seminars, and educational materials to raise awareness about various financial crimes. They empower individuals with the tools and knowledge to recognize and prevent exploitation. They may work in schools, community organizations, or corporate settings to teach individuals about the importance of safeguarding their financial information and making informed decisions.

The fight against financial crimes is a multifaceted endeavor that requires a diverse range of professionals. Whether you're drawn to the intricacies of investigation, the world of cybersecurity, or the realm of legal complexities, there's a role for you to play in safeguarding financial systems and society at large.

By pursuing these careers, you contribute to a safer and more secure financial landscape for all. Your dedication and expertise will be instrumental in preserving the integrity of financial systems and protecting individuals and organizations from exploitation.

CHAPTER THIRTEEN: THE UNITY

In the field of countering financial crimes, it is common to feel overwhelmed by the sheer magnitude of the challenge. However, amidst this chapter, there exists a glimmer of hope and unity. In this chapter, we will mention in a nutshell the worldwide initiatives, organisations, and task forces that are committed to eliminating financial crimes. These collective endeavours serve as evidence that you are not alone in this battle. We unite to create a formidable force against individuals who aim to exploit financial vulnerabilities.

The United Nations plays a crucial role in facilitating international cooperation among nations in combating financial crimes. The Convention against Transnational Organized Crime, commonly referred to as the Palermo Convention, deals with a range of organized criminal activities such as money laundering and corruption. It encourages signatory states to implement measures that strengthen their legal frameworks, thereby enhancing the international response to financial crimes.

The Office on Drugs and Crime (UNODC) of the United Nations takes the lead in combating money laundering, corruption, and illicit financial flows. The United Nations Office on Drugs and Crime (UNODC) offers countries a range of resources, training programs, and technical support to enhance their legal systems and enforcement capabilities.

Also, the Financial Action Task Force (FATF) is an intergovernmental organisation that establishes international standards for combating money laundering and terrorist financing.

The guidance provided by this organisation has a global impact on policies and practices, promoting collaboration among nations to combat financial crime threats effectively.

Task forces on the frontlines play a crucial role in combating financial crimes at both national and regional levels. The U.S. Department of the Treasury's Financial Crimes Enforcement Network (FinCEN), for example, is responsible for collecting and analysing financial data to identify instances of money laundering and other illegal activities.

FinCEN works in collaboration with various law enforcement agencies to effectively disrupt criminal networks and ensure the integrity of the financial system. Also, Europol, which stands for the European Union Agency for Law Enforcement Cooperation, plays a crucial role in promoting collaboration among European countries. The Financial Intelligence Group supports member states in investigating intricate financial crimes by facilitating the exchange of intelligence and expertise.

The organisations and task forces mentioned here are just a small part of the global network that is actively working to combat financial crimes. Numerous professionals, experts, and authorities from around the world contribute their expertise and dedication to this common mission. By collaborating, these entities form a strong defence against financial exploitation. It is equally important to understand the laws and regulations in your own country, in addition to global efforts and to conduct thorough research and become acquainted with the legal framework that governs financial transactions and crimes in your jurisdiction.

Having this knowledge will empower you to make well-informed decisions and take appropriate actions to safeguard both yourself and your finances. We are united in our collective effort to combat financial crimes. Financial systems, rules, and organisations worldwide are collaborating with cybersecurity experts to combat financial crimes. Our goal is to prevent the spread of these harmful actions and minimize their impact. Although we cannot determine the exact timing of our victory, it is evident that without collaboration, we may encounter significant challenges.

SECTION FIVE:
STORY TIME

Welcome to the most thrilling part of our journey! In this section, we'll explore a series of fictional stories crafted to take you on an exciting adventure through the complex world of financial crimes and ethics.

But don't be fooled; these aren't just ordinary tales. Each story, though imagined, is carefully designed to illustrate the core principles, theories, and ideas we've been discussing. These narratives will bring to life the characters, conflicts, and triumphs that could very well exist in the real world. Why are we diving into these fictional stories? Here's why:

- Engaging Exploration: By turning dry facts and concepts into vivid stories, we'll make learning about financial crimes and criminology fun and relatable for you.

- Life Lessons Through Fiction: Each story contains valuable insights and moral lessons. You'll discover the importance of integrity, diligence, and empathy in the face of challenging situations.

- Connecting The Dots: These stories are like pieces of a jigsaw puzzle, helping you see how everything fits together. They make the complex world of finance and crime more approachable.
- A Creative Approach to Learning: By using storytelling, we are engaging your imagination, encouraging you to think critically and fostering a deeper understanding of the subjects at hand.

As you read through these tales, imagine yourself as part of the action. What choices would you make? How would you navigate the challenges faced by the characters? What would you learn from their triumphs and mistakes?

These stories are your playground, a chance to explore ideas and concepts in a safe and engaging way. They're not just entertainment; they're a valuable tool to help you understand, learn, and grow.

Keep in mind that any stories mentioned in this book are meant to be illustrative examples. These stories' characters, events, and scenarios are entirely fictional. Have been created to offer insights into concepts and topics discussed. Any similarities to individuals, whether entities or natural persons are purely coincidental and not intended to represent any specific individual, entity, or situation. The primary objective of these narratives is to promote understanding and engage readers in the matter.

So, let's jump into these stories together and explore a world where finance, ethics, and creativity meet. Get ready for a journey filled with intrigue, excitement, and wisdom!

Story 1: Marcus the Fake Money Maker

During Emperor Nero's reign, a man named Marcus resided in the city of Rome. Renowned throughout the empire for his cunningness and remarkable skills as a forger, Marcus possessed an ability to create coins that closely resembled -- genuine ones. Operating covertly amidst the turmoil of that era, he thrived.

Word spread about Marcus's craftsmanship, and citizens unknowingly began utilizing his coins without knowing the deceit hidden beneath their shiny exteriors. Gradually but steadily, these false coins circulated among the population, sowing seeds of societal confusion and distrust.

They didn't know that this circulation was causing fluctuations in the value of the currency and plunging their stable economy into a state of uncertainty and vulnerability.

Every day that passed, the situation grew more unstable. The economy hovered on the edge of collapse. Marcus's deceit had to have consequences affecting everyone in Rome, from merchants and traders to people. The aftermath was devastating, with families struggling to make ends meet and lives shattered.

However, Marcus's days of mischief came to an end when the Roman government took action against the destabilization of the currency. Determined to uncover the truth behind the coins, skilled detectives and numismatic experts joined forces to pursue justice. Their relentless investigation led them to Marcus's workshop at the city's heart.

In an operation, authorities raided Marcus's workshop. He discovered various tools, Molds, and piles of counterfeit coins, a testament to his deceptive skills. The evidence was undeniable, ultimately leading to Marcus facing the consequences. Summoned before the court, Marcus faced accusations of undermining the foundations of financial stability within the empire. The subsequent trial exposed the extent of his wrongdoing and deceit, creating shockwaves throughout Rome. The era of Marcus's deceit finally ended when the court delivered a verdict that sent a message to anyone who aspires to forge documents; financial deception will not be tolerated.

As news of Marcus's arrest spread, the city breathed a sigh of relief. While still coping with the aftermath of his actions, people found a glimmer of hope for the future. The authorities swiftly intervened to prevent the circulation of coins, which was crucial in stabilizing the Roman economy. Marcu's downfall served as a reminder about the significance of integrity and trust in transactions.

It also sheds light on the reaching consequences that deceptive practices can have on society's social fabric. With the forger now apprehended Rome's citizens learned a lesson about remaining vigilant and safeguarding their currency's integrity.

As the empire worked towards rebuilding its stability Marcuss rise and fall became a tale passed down through generations as a reminder about the repercussions of financial deception. For Romes people it became a lesson in resilience collective responsibility and the ongoing necessity, for financial practices. Thus, the tale of Marcus, the master counterfeiter who almost brought Rome to its downfall emerged as an episode, in the records of Roman history forever engraved as a warning story for future generations. It stood as evidence of the role played by integrity, openness, and responsibility in finance—principles that would continue to shape the trajectory of history for years to follow.

Story 2: Detoured Dreams

Once upon a time there was a man named Alex who lived in a peaceful town. He worked hard. He had dreams for his future. Alex dedicated himself to his studies and extracurricular activities all with the aim of achieving his goal of attending a university.

As the college application deadline approached Alex put in hours to create an application. He carefully crafted a portfolio showcasing his talents and accomplishments. He was confident that his efforts would pay off and pave the way for a future. He Didn't know that corruption had infiltrated the university's admissions process. Mr. Thompson, who oversaw admissions, had formed an alliance with Jakes' father. Despite Jake having grades and fewer achievements than Alex he secured admission through this arrangement.

When Alex received the rejection letter from the university his world crumbled around him. He felt bewildered and heartbroken to discover that despite his performance and unwavering dedication he was overlooked. Driven by a sense of injustice Alex decided to dig into the details of his rejection. Through his investigation he uncovered evidence of Mr. Thompsons collusion with Jakes father, in securing Jakes place at the college through means.

Determined to expose the truth and bring justice to light Alex embarked on a mission to unveil this web of deceit. He collected evidence as he could to prove the corruption, including emails testimonials, from witnesses and records of admissions. With the support of his friends and a local journalist who believed in his cause Alex shared his story with the media.

The story quickly gained traction online sparking anger and putting pressure on the university to investigate the allegations.

In response to mounting evidence and public scrutiny the university administration launched an investigation into the admissions scandal. They implemented reforms in the admissions process to ensure fairness and transparency for applicants. Both Mr. Thompson and Jake's father faced consequences for their actions.

Although Alex missed out on his dream school opportunity his courageous actions served as a catalyst for progress. His story inspired students to take a stand against corruption and fight for educational opportunities.

It became a symbol of resilience and honesty. Through his journey Alex learned lessons about perseverance, truthfulness, and confronting corruption wherever it exists; Despite facing a setback, in life he became an inspiration by demonstrating how integrity and determination can overcome adversity and bring about change.

Story 3: The Weight of Regret

Once upon a time in the city of Newbrook there lived a young man named Chris. He possessed charm and intelligence. Underneath his smile he carried a weight of insecurities. Struggling with difficulties and battling personal demons Chris found himself drawn to the temptation of quick money, through fraudulent means.

One day while exploring the depths of the internet Chris stumbled upon what he believed to be an opportunity that could change his life. With a few clicks he embarked on a dangerous path involving identity theft. Little did he realize that this choice would set off a series of events that would haunt him indefinitely.

Chriss illicit actions led him to cross paths with Mr. Thompson, a retired schoolteacher who had invested his life savings in securing a bright future for his only son Alex. Alex was suffering from a liver condition that required urgent surgery to save his life.

Unaware of the reaching consequences of his actions Chris manipulated his way into Mr. Thompsons financial accounts. The funds intended to provide for Alexs's surgery ended up in Chriss possession instead leaving Mr. Thompson devastated and feeling utterly helpless. The surgery was postponed due to a lack of funds, which led to Alexs's condition deteriorating and the hope dwindling with each passing day.

Unfortunately, the surgery never took place. Alexs fragile body succumbed to his illness leaving Mr. Thompson. Inconsolable. The weight of guilt crashed down on Chriss shoulders like a burden. He realized that his selfish actions had caused the loss of a life, tormented his conscience, and robbed him of sleep.

Haunted by guilt and remorse Chris made a life-changing decision. He chose to distance himself from the world of fraud, determined to make amends, for the pain he had inflicted. However even as he left his past behind nightmares continued to plague him.

The faces of Mr. Thompson and memories of Alex haunted his sleep relentlessly serving as reminders of the irreparable harm he had caused. Chris dedicated his days to seeking redemption by volunteering at community centers and supporting causes. Nonetheless the internal anguish never truly subsided. The weight of guilt remained a present companion reminding him that certain wounds could never fully heal.

Ultimately Chriss story serves as a reminder that even one act of fraud can have far reaching consequences. His transformation from being deceived to feeling remorse showcases the influence of human decisions and the lasting effects they have on our lives.

Story 4: Heart-Broken Emily

Once upon a time, in a small town, lived a teenager named Emily. She was known for her kind heart, eagerness to help others, and passion for photography. One day, while browsing online, Emily stumbled upon an advertisement for a prestigious photography competition that promised fame and fortune. Excited by the opportunity, she clicked on the link and entered her personal information.

Little did Emily know that the advertisement was a cleverly crafted fraud scheme. Unbeknownst to her, her personal information was now in the hands of cunning scammers. Over the next few weeks, Emily started receiving calls and emails from unknown individuals posing as representatives of the photography competition. They congratulated her on being selected as a finalist and offered her a chance to secure her spot by paying a hefty fee. In her excitement and desire for success, Emily fell victim to their persuasive tactics. She paid the fee, eagerly anticipating her moment of triumph. However, as days turned into weeks, she realised something was amiss. The photography competition she eagerly believed in was nothing more than a facade.

Heartbroken and betrayed, Emily realised she had become a victim of fraud. She felt a mixture of anger, regret and vulnerability. The scammers had stolen her hard-earned money and shattered her dreams of recognition and success.

But Emily refused to let this experience define her. Determined to fight back, she reported the fraud to the authorities, warning them of the scam to protect others from falling into the same trap. Through her resilience and courage, she learned the importance of skepticism, research, and verifying the legitimacy of opportunities before taking any action.

This experience became a turning point in Emily's life. She channeled her disappointment and frustration into educating herself and others about the dangers of fraud. Through her photography and storytelling, she created awareness campaigns, sharing her story and inspiring others to be vigilant, cautious, and skeptical of offers that seemed too good to be true.

Emily's journey taught her the value of resilience, critical thinking, and the power of using her voice to make a difference. She emerged more robust and determined to pursue her dreams while keeping fraudsters at bay. Her story reminds teenagers everywhere to stay informed, trust their instincts, and never let their aspirations prevent them from recognising potential scams.

Story 5: The Enigmatic Scam

Once upon a time in the town of St. Lucia there resided a bright and ambitious teenager named Sophia. She was renowned for her spirit and eagerness to explore new experiences. Sophias world brimmed with curiosity and excitement; however, little did she suspect that her thirst for adventure would entangle her in a deception.

On one afternoon Sophia received an intriguing email from an individual who identified themselves as Prince Alexander claiming to be a wealthy European prince. The message detailed Prince Alexanders need for her assistance in claiming an inheritance left by a distant relative. Intrigued by the prospect of aiding royalty and captivated by the unknown that lay ahead, Sophia responded to the email blissfully unaware of the web she was about to enter.

As their correspondence unfolded Prince Alexander skillfully wove an enchanting narrative, about his opulence and the immense fortune awaiting him. To facilitate the transfer of these inherited funds he requested Sophia's banking information and personal details. Blinded by the allure of wealth and longing to be part of something extraordinary Sophia naively shared her information. Before long, peculiar events began unfolding in Sophia's life. Her bank account became plagued with charges while simultaneously receiving threatening messages from unidentified sources.

Her happy and carefree world took a dark turn, becoming filled with fear and uncertainty. Worried for her safety Sophia confided in her kind and wise neighbor, Mr. Thomas, who happened to be a retired police officer. Mr. Thomas attentively listened to Sophias story. She quickly recognized the signs of a classic fraudulent scheme.

With Mr. Thomas as her guide Sophia made the decision to take action against the cunning scammer. Together they reported the activity to the local authorities and the cybercrime department. The police initiated an investigation into the matter diligently tracing the footprints left by the scammer.

While this was unfolding Sophia learned a lesson about skepticism and caution in our digital age. She came to realize that not everything that shines are gold; she needed to remain vigilant and discerning when dealing with strangers online.

As time went by law enforcement successfully tracked down and apprehended the scammer. It was revealed that Prince Alexander was nothing than an imposter—a seasoned fraudster who had duped numerous innocent victims before crossing paths with Sophia. Thanks to her act of reporting the crime countless others were saved from falling into his trap. In the end Sophia emerged from this experience more robust and wiser than before.

Story 6: Patriot Ryan

Once upon a time there was a man named Ryan who lived in a peaceful part of town. Ryan was like any other high school student, full of dreams and aspirations. Little did he know that his life was about to take a turn.

One day while going about his routine Ryan crossed paths with Chris, a friendly and seemingly trustworthy stranger. Chriss amiable nature instantly made him famous among Ryans friends. As their friendship grew stronger Ryan felt opening up to Chris about his hopes and dreams.

Unrecognized, Ryan Chris had a motive. He was a member of a terrorist organization. Their plan involved deceiving people and acquiring funds for their activities. For Ryan his innocence and eagerness to contribute to something meaningful made him the perfect target.

Gradually Chris started introducing ideas and extremist beliefs into Ryans mindset. Through harmless conversations and sharing of information he skillfully manipulated Ryan without raising suspicion.

Following Chriss guidance Ryan unwittingly began engaging in activities that provided support to the terrorist group. He got entangled in their scheme through online transactions and fundraising events. Eventually as time passed by doubts started creeping into Ryans mind. He began sensing that something was not quite right...He started questioning Chriss motives when he urged him to engage in dangerous activities. Down he felt the need to break free from being manipulated.

Ryan found the determination to distance himself from Chris and seek guidance from adults in his life. They collaborated to uncover Chriss reasons and report them to the authorities. Ryans courage played a role, in disrupting the network that financed terrorists and preventing any further entanglement on his part.

Story 7: Lily the Innocent

Once upon a time there was a teenager named Lily who lived in the vibrant city of Verityville. She had gained quite a reputation for her tech skills and her passion for online gaming.

She didn't know that her extraordinary abilities would attract the attention of an individual involved in illegal money activities. It all started on a day when Lily was taking part in an international gaming tournament. At that moment she caught the eye of a player known only as "ShadowMaster." This mysterious person reached out to Lily luring her with a proposition.

Unaware of ShadowMaster's intentions Lily was drawn into his web of deceit as he posed as a mentor figure. Gradually ShadowMaster introduced Lily to what seemed like an online trading platform promising significant financial rewards.

He asked her to collect $200 from someone she didn't know and then keep $50 for herself while making some genuine purchases on his platform using the remaining balance. He reassured her that these purchases were simply for testing purposes. ShadowMaster explained that he chose people he trusted for this task offering the $50 as a reward for each contribution made during this specific period to assess the transaction process on his platform.

Little did Lily know that the platform she was using had an agenda. To launder money acquired from street level drug dealing. Unaware of the side Lily fell into ShadowMaster's trap, enticed by the promise of quick and easy cash. Everything started innocently when Lilys parents provided her with a Betty cash debit card for her allowance at the age of 14.

Little did they know that it would pave the way for Lily to unknowingly participate in ShadowMaster's money laundering scheme through transactions on this platform. Under the disguise of gaming Lily, she unknowingly turned illegal funds into seemingly legitimate assets. However, fate had plans in store for her. Agent Phoenix, a cybercrime investigator had been closely monitoring ShadowMaster's activities and stumbled upon Lilys involvement. To protect her Agent Phoenix intervened by conducting surveillance and gathering valuable intelligence.

Story 8: The Resilient Canvas

In a city known for its creativity and innovative spirit there lived Aisha, a talented artist. With her imagination and expert craftsmanship, she dedicatedly created artworks that resonated deeply with people worldwide. Her creations did not provide her with a source of income. It also stood as a testament to her unwavering passion and dedication.

One day, while browsing the platform where she showcased her work, Aisha stumbled upon something that shattered her heart. She discovered a website that was offering her artwork for download without seeking any permission from her. The realization hit her like a wave. All those hours of hard work, the immense creativity she poured into each piece and the dreams associated with them were being exploited by digital pirates.

A mix of frustration and anger surged within Aisha as she delved deeper into the realm of piracy. She uncovered instances where not her artwork but also creations by countless other artists were unlawfully reproduced and distributed without any shame or remorse.

These pirates shamelessly profited from stolen content while leaving creators like Aisha in straits.

Continuing her research on this distressing issue Aisha came across heart wrenching stories shared by artists who had endured ordeals. Some had even been forced to abandon their pursuits due to the financial burden imposed by rampant piracy.

thers discussed the impact they felt when their work was used without their consent, leaving them with a sense of violation and helplessness.

Aisha, determined to make a difference, teamed up with artists to fight against piracy. Together they launched campaigns to raise awareness about the effects of piracy on artists livelihoods and the broader creative industry.

Their hard work gained attention from both the media and the public, shedding light on this overlooked issue and its consequences.

Aisha's group committed themselves to educating people about the importance of supporting content and respecting artists' rights. They collaborated with experts to explore ways to combat piracy. They also encouraged fans to report instances of piracy and advocate for compensation for artists.

Their campaign gained momentum. It started yielding results as internet users began recognizing the significance of respecting copyrights and supporting artists by purchasing their work. Additionally, government bodies and online platforms took notice.

They have implemented measures to prevent piracy while ensuring that artists receive earnings. Over time Aishas efforts paid off as the landscape of piracy began to change giving renewed hope to aspiring artists like her in their fight, for rights.

Through their efforts, they did not protect their interests but also fostered a culture that valued creativity and originality. Aishas journey, from being a victim of piracy to becoming an advocate showcases the power of artists uniting to safeguard their art their means of living and the future of expression, in the age.

Story 9: The Guardian of Truth

Once upon a time, a curious and ambitious teenager named Amir lived in the vibrant city of Hadiya. He had always been fascinated by the world of finance and dreamed of positively impacting his community. His parents, Nadia, and Khalid were hardworking individuals who had instilled strong values of honesty and integrity in their son.

One day, Amir's best friend, Hasan, introduced him to a new investment opportunity. Hasan claimed that it was a foolproof way to double their money quickly and support local businesses in need. Intrigued by the prospect of helping others and seeing his wealth grow, Amir decided to invest some of his savings. As the days passed, Amir noticed some unusual patterns. Hasan lived a lavish lifestyle, indulging in expensive gadgets and luxurious outings. When Amir asked about Hasan's newfound wealth source, he brushed it off, saying he had stumbled upon a lucky streak of investments. However, Amir couldn't shake off the feeling that something was amiss.

His instinct told him to investigate further, especially after hearing whispers in the community about financial scams that had affected several families. As he delved deeper into the investment scheme, he discovered it was a fraudulent Ponzi scheme. Faced with this shocking revelation, Amir confronted Hasan about the truth. Initially defensive, Hasan finally confessed to falling prey to a twisted creed of easy money and dishonesty. He had become a pawn in a much larger scheme orchestrated by cunning individuals who exploited vulnerable teenagers like himself.

Realising the gravity of his mistake, Amir made a tough decision to sever ties with Hasan and report the fraudulent scheme to the authorities. Although he had lost some of his hard-earned money, he knew that exposing the criminals was right. He also warned his family and friends about the dangers of falling into the trap of financial crimes and the importance of thoroughly researching opportunities. The community was shocked and grateful for Amir's bravery in speaking out as the truth came to light.

His actions protected others from falling victim to the scam and taught everyone a valuable lesson about the importance of being cautious and informed about finances. Amir's determination to seek the truth and his commitment to integrity earned him the respect and admiration of his family and peers. He learned that true success and prosperity come from making honest choices and valuing the well-being of others above personal gain.

From that day forward, Amir dedicated himself to spreading awareness about financial crimes and empowering his fellow teenagers to make smart financial decisions. He knew they could build a future without deception and financial hardships by acquiring knowledge and critical thinking.

And so, the story of Amir became a beacon of hope and inspiration for the young generation of Hadiya City, reminding them that in the face of twisted creeds and dishonest schemes, one's unwavering integrity and dedication to truth could make all the difference.

Story 10: Title: Shadows of Deception

In the heart of a bustling city, far away from prying eyes, a hidden empire of crime flourished. Antonio Marino, a mastermind in the world of money laundering, operated discreetly within the shadows. His source of funds was a thriving drug trade, which brought in immense profits but needed a way to be "cleaned."

Antonio devised a complex scheme to launder illicit gains. He started by opening a chain of seemingly legitimate cash-intensive businesses: a string of laundromats, small cafes, and car washes scattered around the city. These businesses handled a high volume of cash transactions, making them perfect vehicles for his operation.

Step one involved mingling the drug money with the legitimate earnings from these businesses. Every day, stacks of cash from the drug trade found their way into the cash registers of Antonio's establishments. But to outsiders, these cash flows appeared entirely normal, as they were often masked by genuine earnings.

Step two was layering. Antonio transferred funds between his various businesses using a web of bank accounts. He also introduced dummy companies to confuse the paper trail further. As the money moved through multiple transactions, it became increasingly difficult to trace its origins. Bank transfers, shell corporations, and transactions across international borders further obscured the illicit source.

The final step was integration. Antonio invested the "cleaned" money into real estate, luxury goods, and legitimate investments. He purchased upscale properties under different names, filled his garages with luxury cars, and even dabbled in art. The assets he acquired were not only valuable but also easily transferable and difficult to seize.

Over time, Antonio's empire grew, and he managed to evade law enforcement's radar due to the intricacies of his operation. His lavish lifestyle and outwardly successful businesses masked the darkness that fueled his wealth. However, the shadows couldn't hide the truth forever. As law enforcement agencies honed their skills in tracking financial irregularities, they gradually unraveled Antonio's elaborate scheme. A joint effort across borders exposed his empire, and he was apprehended.

Antonio's story serves as a cautionary tale, shedding light on the sinister world of money laundering. It teaches us the importance of vigilant financial oversight, the need to close regulatory loopholes, and the power of international cooperation to combat these illicit activities.

Story 11: The Spider Web

In a bustling city known for its luxury and glamour, a man named Alex found himself entangled in a world of crime and deception. Alex had amassed significant wealth through his illegal drug trade operations. However, he knew that directly using the proceeds from his criminal activities could lead to suspicion and investigation. So, he devised a plan to launder his ill-gotten gains and make them appear legitimate.

Stage 1: Placement: Alex's first step was to place his dirty money into the legitimate financial system. He chose to visit local businesses and casinos, where he converted his stacks of cash into chips and tokens. These establishments had high cash turnovers, making it difficult to trace the origins of the money.

Stage 2: Layering: With his casino winnings in hand, Alex embarked on the layering phase. He began transferring funds between offshore accounts using complex transactions involving multiple banks and intermediaries. These transactions created a convoluted paper trail, making it challenging for authorities to track the money's source.

Stage 3: Integration: Alex now needed to integrate his laundered funds into the legitimate economy.

He established a shell company that purported to engage in legitimate business activities, such as real estate investment. Using his illicit funds, he purchased properties through the shell company.

These transactions created the appearance of legal income and wealth. Eventually, he wanted to enjoy his "clean" money without raising suspicion. He repatriated the funds back into his home country and used them to purchase luxury cars, upscale properties, and high-end jewelry. He also invested in legitimate businesses, portraying himself as a successful entrepreneur.

Unbeknownst to Alex, his activities did not go unnoticed. Law enforcement agencies and financial investigators were meticulously tracking his movements. Eventually, they gathered enough evidence to link his extravagant purchases and investments to his illegal drug trade. In a dramatic turn of events, Alex's world came crashing down when he was apprehended by the authorities. His intricate money laundering scheme had been exposed, leading to his arrest and the seizure of his ill-gotten assets. The story served as a stark reminder of the serious consequences of money laundering and the determined efforts of law enforcement to combat financial crimes.

Story 12: A Tale of Shell

In the bustling city of Metropolis, beneath the glitzy facade of corporate skyscrapers and lavish lifestyles, a sinister scheme was unfolding. This is the story of how a seemingly innocuous shell company became a central player in an elaborate money laundering operation.

Meet Alex Thompson, a cunning mastermind with a penchant for manipulation. Alex had successfully orchestrated a network of illegal activities, from drug trafficking to extortion, amassing a vast fortune in illicit funds. However, Alex knew that keeping this fortune hidden was the key to staying one step ahead of the law.

To accomplish this, Alex turned to an old acquaintance, Vanessa Miller, a financial consultant with connections to the underworld. Together, they hatched a plan that involved the creation of a shell company named "Prestige Holdings Inc." The purpose of this company? To provide the perfect cover for their money laundering activities.

Vanessa skillfully navigated through the labyrinth of legal procedures, registering Prestige Holdings Inc. in an offshore tax haven known for its lenient regulations and discreet financial services. With the company established, Alex transferred his ill-gotten gains into the accounts of Prestige Holdings Inc., effectively masking the origin of the funds. Next, Vanessa orchestrated a series of transactions between Prestige Holdings Inc. and legitimate businesses, carefully manipulating the flow of money to create confusion and obfuscate the paper trail. Fake invoices, overvalued contracts, and phantom services became the tools of their trade. As the transactions increased, the funds moved seamlessly between accounts, both domestic and international. Alex and Vanessa capitalized on the complexities of the financial system, utilizing shell companies, dummy corporations, and offshore accounts to ensure the funds' invisibility to prying eyes.

Months passed, and Alex's illegal wealth was now buried beneath layers of deception. With the authorities clueless and his operation seemingly untraceable, he revealed in his success. However, the tide was about to turn.

Enter Detective Maya Patel, a tenacious investigator known for her relentless pursuit of justice. Suspicion had arisen about the sudden wealth fluctuations within legitimate businesses connected to Prestige Holdings Inc. She embarked on a mission to unveil the truth, following the money's convoluted path with determination. Her painstaking efforts led her to uncover the intricate web of shell companies, money transfers, and falsified documents that had shielded Alex's ill-gotten fortune. Armed with evidence, she presented her findings to a team of financial experts and law enforcement officials.

In a dramatic turn of events, search warrants were executed, and Vanessa was apprehended. Under intense questioning, she disclosed the elaborate money laundering scheme, exposing the manipulation behind Prestige Holdings Inc. Alex's empire of deceit was unravelling. The subsequent trial became a spectacle, showcasing the devastating consequences of money laundering. Alex was ultimately convicted of his crimes, and Vanessa faced justice as well.

Their story served as a cautionary tale of the dangers of shell company money laundering, illustrating how layers of deception can be dismantled by dedicated individuals seeking to uphold the law. The tale of Prestige Holdings Inc. stands as a testament to the persistence of those who strive to expose hidden truths and dismantle the intricate webs that criminals weave to obscure their illegal activities.

Story 13: Doing the Right Wrong

Once upon a time, a teenager named Michael lived in a peaceful town. He was a kind-hearted and ambitious young man with dreams of making a difference in the world. He believed in the power of compassion, unity, and spreading love to those who needed it most. However, tragedy struck when Michael's path crossed with evil extremists who exploited his vulnerabilities and manipulated his beliefs in the name of religious ideologies. In their twisted version of faith, they preached hatred and violence, preying on innocent minds like Michael's.

As their influence tightened its grip on him, Michael noticed some troubling red flags hinting at his dangerous path. Deep down, he knew what he was doing was illegal and that the signs pointed to something more sinister. But the extremists were skilled at deception, convincing him that the money he was collecting would be used to support low-income families in need. Michael ignored the alarming signs because he wanted to help the less fortunate and kept raising money. He believed he was doing the right thing, unaware of the hidden agenda behind the façade of benevolence.

He didn't know that the money he collected was not destined for those in need. Instead, it was funneled into financing weapons, providing the extremists with the means to carry out a horrific act of mass killing. Lives were lost, families were shattered, and a deep sense of sorrow engulfed the town. The devastating consequences of his actions weighed heavily on Michael's conscience. The realization of his unwitting participation in such a tragedy consumed him with guilt and remorse.

He struggled to comprehend how he had been so easily manipulated, and the weight of responsibility crushed his spirit, so he decided to turn himself in and tell everything. As justice unfolded, Michael was convicted and sentenced to 10 years for his role in the terrorist act. The weight of his sentence mirrored the weight of the lives lost as he grappled with the consequences of his actions behind bars. Michael embarked on a journey of self-reflection and redemption within the confines of the prison walls. He dedicated himself to understanding the depths of his mistakes and vowed to spend the rest of his life fighting against the ideologies that had led him astray.

With the guidance of prison counsellors, Michael underwent intensive rehabilitation programs that helped him confront his past and gain a deeper understanding of the manipulation tactics employed by extremist groups. He used this newfound knowledge to become an advocate for countering radicalisation and preventing vulnerable individuals from falling into the same trap.

Through letters and outreach programs, Michael shared his story with other young people, urging them to question ideologies and resist the allure of those who seek to exploit their beliefs. He symbolized hope and resilience, demonstrating that redemption and positive change were possible even in the darkest times.

As he served his sentence, Michael dedicated himself to spreading awareness about the dangers of radicalisation and the devastating consequences it could have on individuals, families, and communities. He collaborated with organisations working to counter extremism and actively participated in deradicalization programs within the prison system.

Michael's journey serves as a cautionary tale and a testament to the power of personal transformation. Through his own tragic experience, he emerged as a force for good, working tirelessly to prevent others from falling prey to the twisted ideologies that had led him astray. While he could never undo the pain he had caused, he made it his life's mission to ensure that others would not follow the same destructive path. In the end, Michael's story serves as a reminder that the web of extremism can ensnare even the most well-intentioned people. It underscores the importance of critical thinking, education, and resilience in the face of manipulation. Through his efforts, Michael sought to create a world where vulnerable minds were shielded from the clutches of extremism and where forgiveness and redemption could pave the way for a brighter future.

Story 14: The Illusion of Friendship

Once upon a time, a teenager named Mark lived in a quiet neighborhood. He had a best friend named John, and they were inseparable. They shared many adventures, dreams, and even financial matters. Little did Mark know that his friendship with John would take an unexpected turn. John was a charismatic and charming friend, but he had a hidden secret. He had gotten into much debt and struggled to make ends meet. However, he knew just how much Mark cared for him and saw an opportunity to exploit their friendship for his gain.

One day, John approached Mark with a plea for help. He said he urgently needed money to pay off his debts. His caring friend Mark agreed to lend John the money without asking too many questions. Weeks passed, and John's financial situation seemed to improve dramatically. He started living a lavish lifestyle beyond what a typical teenager could afford. Expensive clothes, fancy gadgets, and luxurious outings became a part of John's daily life.

As Mark observed this sudden change, he couldn't help but wonder how John managed to repay his debts and afford such a lifestyle. However, whenever Mark brought up the topic, John would change the subject or provide vague explanations. Despite the doubts in his mind, Mark continued to support his friend financially, convinced that he was doing the right thing. After all, they were best friends, and Mark wanted to help John in any way he could.

Little did Mark know that John's newfound wealth needed to be acquired legitimately. John had involved himself in illegal activities, such as identity theft and fraud, to maintain his extravagant lifestyle. He saw Mark's trust to an end, using their friendship to finance his illicit actions.

The truth eventually came to light when the authorities caught up with John's criminal activities. Mark was left shocked and betrayed, realising that his friend had deceived him all along. He couldn't believe the person he trusted had used their friendship for such unethical purposes.

Mark was caught in the middle of the investigation, questioned by the authorities, and faced the consequences of his association with John. Though he was innocent of wrongdoing, Mark deeply regretted his blind trust and that he unknowingly enabled John's criminal behaviour.

This experience served as a profound lesson for Mark. It taught him the importance of being cautious, even with those closest to you. He realised the need to question and verify the actions of others, especially when it involves money or suspicious behaviours. Mark vowed to be more discerning in his relationships, to trust his instincts, and never again to fall prey to deception in the name of friendship.

Story 15: Alone in a Sea of Doubt

In a quiet neighborhood, she lived a teenager named Mia. She was excited to start her summer vacation, planning to hang out with her friends and explore the city. Little did she know that a simple mistake would change her life.

One day, Mia received a text message claiming to be from her bank. It said her account had been compromised and she needed to confirm her details urgently. Panicked, she followed the instructions and provided her personal information. Unbeknownst to her, it was a scam.

Weeks later, Mia noticed unusual transactions on her bank statement. Her heart sank as she realized she had been tricked. She felt a mix of anger, shame, and fear. Afraid of admitting her mistake to her friends, she withdrew from social gatherings. She couldn't shake the feeling that they would judge her for falling for such a scam. As days turned into weeks, Mia's isolation grew. She spent more time alone, avoiding her friends' calls and messages. She felt like a burden, worried that they would think less of her for being a victim. Even though she longed for their support, the shame kept her at a distance.

One afternoon, Mia's best friend, Alex, knocked on her door. Concerned by Mia's sudden absence, Alex wanted to check in. Mia hesitated before finally opening up about what had happened. To her surprise, Alex listened without judgment and shared her own stories of times she'd been fooled online. As Mia realized she wasn't alone, a weight lifted off her shoulders. She realized that everyone could make mistakes, and it doesn't define who they are. Slowly, she began reconnecting with her friends and rebuilding her social life.

Mia's experience taught her that hiding her struggles only made her feel more isolated. Opening up about her vulnerability led to understanding, empathy, and stronger connections with those who cared about her. And as she embraced her imperfections, she helped break down the stigma surrounding financial crimes, showing that anyone could be a victim.

Story 16: Shattered Trust, Healing Hearts

In a quaint neighborhood, they lived a retired couple, Grace and Robert. They had spent decades saving for their dream vacation, a cross-country road trip they had always wanted. Their excitement was palpable as they embarked on their journey, but little did they know that their trust would soon be shattered.

During their road trip, Grace received a call from their bank informing her of suspicious activity on their account. Panic washed over her as she checked their balance online. Their entire savings, resulting from years of hard work and sacrifice, had vanished. The couple's joyful adventure turned into a nightmare.

Devastated, Grace and Robert returned home and immediately contacted the authorities. As they recounted the events to the police and financial investigators, their emotions swung wildly between anger, frustration, and disbelief. Realizing that someone had taken advantage of their trust and stolen their savings, they felt violated.

Days turned into weeks, and the couple immersed themselves in legal proceedings to recover their funds. The stress of dealing with lawyers, paperwork, and uncertainty took a toll on their mental well-being. Sleepless nights became the norm, and their once-closed bond began to fray under the weight of their emotional distress.

One evening, a neighbor named Sarah noticed their plight and decided to reach out. She had heard about their situation and wanted them to offer her support. Over a cup of tea, Grace and Robert opened up about their feelings of helplessness and frustration. Sarah listened empathetically, sharing her own stories of overcoming adversity.

Sarah's compassion and understanding provided a glimmer of hope for Grace and Robert. She connected them with a support group of other victims who had experienced similar financial crimes. Through sharing their stories and leaning on each other, they found solace in knowing they weren't alone in their struggles.

As the legal process continued, Grace and Robert's emotions began to stabilize. With the guidance of their support group and Sarah's unwavering friendship, they slowly rebuilt their lives. While the scars of their ordeal remained, they learned to cope with their emotions and focus on rebuilding their financial security.

Story 17: The Frayed Threads of Trust

In the tranquil neighborhood of Willowbrook, where houses with white picket fences exuded an air of warmth and camaraderie, lived an elderly widow named Mrs. Thompson. Widely regarded as the heart of the community, her front porch was adorned with colorful flowers, and her door was always open to anyone in need of advice, a cup of tea, or a comforting word. Her savings, meticulously accumulated over years of hard work and frugality, were her pride a testament to her resilience and diligence.

One crisp morning, as sunlight painted the streets golden,

Mrs. Thompson received an unexpected call from a man named Robert. With a charming demeanor and an air of conviction, he identified himself as a representative of a reputable charity that aimed to support elderly citizens in need. With empathy in his voice, he spoke passionately about the organisation's mission, sharing heartwarming stories of how others had generously contributed to the cause. He assured Mrs. Thompson that her donation, no matter the amount, would make a substantial impact on improving the lives of seniors in the community.

Moved by the cause and the charismatic nature of the caller, Mrs. Thompson agreed to contribute a significant portion of her savings. She felt a sense of purpose and pride, believing that her generosity would indeed bring positive change. Weeks turned into months, and as time flowed like a gentle river, Mrs. Thompson noticed something deeply unsettling— her life savings were depleting at an alarming rate. What was once a nest egg that brought her comfort is now a source of distress and anxiety.

As investigations later revealed, the charity Robert represented was a cruel facade, a fraudulent scheme masterminded by criminals. Mrs. Thompson's hard-earned money had vanished into a void of deception, leaving her financially devastated and emotionally wounded. The news rippled through Willowbrook like a shockwave, triggering a wave of collective anger and betrayal. The very trust that had woven the fabric of this close-knit community was now unravelling.

Neighbors, who had once shared smiles and stories, now exchanged wary glances. The harmony that had been the hallmark of Willowbrook was fractured, and palpable tension lingered in the air. The incident cast a shadow over the spirit of the neighborhood, a haunting reminder that even the most genuine intentions could be exploited by those seeking to sow discord. The trust that had bound them together was now frayed, revealing the vulnerability that lay beneath the surface.

Story 18: The Uneven Scales of Wealth

In the bustling heart of the metropolis known as "Prosper," where towering skyscrapers reached for the heavens and the symphony of car horns and bustling crowds was ever-present, lived a young artist named Carlos. His small studio, tucked away in the labyrinthine alleys of the city, was a sanctuary of creativity and inspiration. With a paintbrush in hand, he brought to life vibrant scenes that mirrored the city's dichotomy—a juxtaposition of grandeur and disparity.

Carlos possessed a rare gift, one that allowed him to capture the essence of life's beauty and struggles on the canvas. His paintings were a testament to his unwavering spirit and a reflection of his observations of both the opulence and the struggles that defined "Prosper." He lived in the bustling district, surrounded by towering skyscrapers that seemed to scrape the sky, while the less fortunate dwelled in the shadows of prosperity.

Despite his undeniable talent, Carlos's harsh reality-based circumstances frequently overshadowed his dreams. "Prospera's" wealth was evident, but so was its price—financial crimes that thrived on the margins of affluence. The city's gleaming facade masked a deep-rooted disparity that seemed to widen with each passing day. The relentless pursuit of wealth had spawned a culture of exploitation and inequality, leaving some to thrive while others barely survived.

One day, as Carlos was strolling through the busy streets, he noticed an opulent gala that the city's elite were hosting. Crystal chandeliers sparkled, and laughter echoed through the air as extravagance took centre stage. The stark contrast between the lavish event and the hardships he witnessed daily struck him like a bolt of lightning. The glaring divide between the haves and the have-nots was an affront to his artistic sensibilities, igniting a fire within him.

In his small studio, Carlos began to paint with a fervor he had never felt before. His canvases transformed into powerful statements that challenged the status quo, spotlighting the inequity that financial crimes had unleashed upon Prosper. His art became a rallying cry, an embodiment of the collective frustrations of those who were overshadowed by opulence. His work resonated deeply, sparking conversations about systemic change and the urgent need to level the playing field. Carlos's art fueled a movement that transcended class boundaries, uniting the city's diverse residents for a common cause. The movement demanded transparency, accountability, and an end to the unchecked financial crimes that perpetuated inequality. Through his art, Carlos ignited a conversation that had long been stifled.

Story 19: Stolen Identity

Lucas was on top of the world. At 16, he had just received his first-ever credit card, a symbol of newfound independence. He felt grown-up, mature, and ready to take on the world. The shiny piece of plastic in his wallet opened doors to online shopping, something he'd longed to explore without needing to borrow his parents' cards.

His friends were equally excited, often gathering around his phone as he browsed through online stores. Lucas was cautious with his spending but loved the sense of freedom his credit card provided.

One day, Lucas stumbled upon an advertisement for a new social media platform that was quickly becoming the next big thing among teenagers. Intrigued and wanting to be part of the trend, he eagerly signed up. As he filled out the online form, he noticed an option for a "premium membership." All it required was his credit card information, something he hadn't thought twice about providing. Weeks passed, and Lucas enjoyed the perks of the new platform, connecting with friends and following the latest trends. Life went on, and the excitement of the new social media site became part of his daily routine.

Then, one ordinary afternoon, Lucas's world was turned

upside down. He opened his credit card statement to find charges for items he had never purchased. Expensive gadgets, designer clothes, subscriptions to unknown services – all listed, one after another. Panicking, he ran to his parents, who immediately called the bank. An investigation was launched, and the family spent agonizing days waiting for news. Meanwhile, Lucas felt a mixture of emotions – fear, anger, shame, and a gnawing sense that he had let his family down.

The investigation revealed the shocking truth: the social media platform Lucas had trusted was a facade. Behind its sleek design and engaging content lay a criminal operation, harvesting personal information from unsuspecting teenagers like Lucas. His identity had been stolen; his credit card information sold to the highest bidder.

Though the bank eventually reversed the charges, the experience left deep scars on Lucas. He became wary of sharing personal information online and withdrew from social media platforms he had once enjoyed. His friends were supportive but couldn't fully understand the magnitude of his experience. It was a personal journey, a path that led Lucas to become more cautious and aware of the risks lurking in the digital world.

The story of Lucas's stolen identity became a cautionary tale, not just for him but for his friends and family. A simple mistake had led to a complex web of deception and betrayal, forever changing his perspective on trust and security in the online world.

Story 20: The Phishing Trip

Nina, an enthusiastic 17-year-old, was always looking for ways to save money for college. She'd taken on part-time jobs, cut back on unnecessary expenses, and kept a close eye on her savings account. Every penny counted, and she knew that her hard work would pay off when it was time to head off to university.

One day, as she was scrolling through her emails, she

stumbled upon a message from her bank. The subject line caught her eye: "Urgent Security Alert: Verify Your Account Now!" Nina's heart skipped a beat. She clicked the email, her mind racing with thoughts of what could be wrong.

The email looked official, complete with the bank's logo, formal language, and even a link to what appeared to be the bank's website. It stated that her account had been compromised and that immediate action was required to verify her information.

Without hesitating, Nina clicked the link, anxious to resolve the issue. The webpage looked just like her bank's login page. She entered her username and password, followed by some personal information, believing she was taking the necessary steps to secure her account.

Days went by, and Nina forgot about the email. Life carried on as usual, filled with schoolwork, friends, and part-time shifts at the local café. Then, one morning, Nina checked her bank account and froze in disbelief. Her savings, the money she had worked so hard to accumulate, was gone. Panic set in as she called her bank, her voice trembling as she explained the situation.

The bank's representative listened carefully and then delivered the devastating news: Nina had fallen victim to a phishing scam. The email wasn't from her bank at all. The link had directed her to a fraudulent website, designed to look like her bank's login page. The thieves had used the information she provided to access her account and steal her savings. The following weeks were a blur of paperwork, phone calls, and meetings with the bank's fraud department. Nina's parents were supportive, but the sense of betrayal and violation weighed heavily on her.

Though the bank managed to recover some of the stolen funds, Nina's trust in the digital world was shattered. The email that had seemed so genuine was a carefully crafted trap, a lure that had drawn her into a web of deceit. The experience became a defining moment in Nina's life, a harsh reminder that not everything online is what it seems. She vowed to be more vigilant, to question, and to verify, knowing that her hard-earned money was a valuable target for those lurking in the shadows of the internet.

Story 21: The Gift Card Scam

Tommy, a 15-year-old with a passion for technology, was thrilled when he landed a part-time job at a popular electronics store in his town. Surrounded by gadgets and gizmos, he couldn't have asked for a better place to work. He quickly became friends with his coworkers and prided himself on his knowledge of the latest tech trends.

One busy Saturday, a well-dressed man approached Tommy at the counter, introducing himself as a businessman from out of town. He explained that he needed to purchase a large number of gift cards for a corporate event and had chosen this store because of its reputation.

Tommy was flattered and eager to help. The man's request seemed straightforward: he wanted to buy fifty gift cards, each loaded with $100. He even offered to pay in cash, presenting a thick envelope filled with crisp bills.

As Tommy began processing the transaction, the man engaged him in friendly conversation, asking about his interests, school, and future plans. Tommy found himself drawn to the charismatic stranger, sharing stories and laughing at his jokes. Once the transaction was complete, the man thanked Tommy warmly, shook his hand, and left the store, leaving Tommy with a sense of accomplishment.

The next day, the store manager called Tommy into his office. His face was stern, and Tommy could tell that something was wrong. The manager explained that the gift cards sold the previous day had been used in an online scam. The police were involved, and the store was facing potential legal issues.

Tommy's heart sank. He had been duped, manipulated by a smooth-talking stranger who had used his trust to commit a crime. He felt ashamed, naive, and utterly defeated. The following weeks were difficult for Tommy. He cooperated with the police, providing details about the man and the transaction. He faced questioning from his coworkers, some sympathetic, others judgmental. The once-enjoyable job had become a source of stress and anxiety.

Eventually, the man was caught, and it was revealed that he was part of a larger criminal ring that used gift cards to launder money. Though Tommy was not held responsible, the experience left a lasting impact on him.

He realized that even the most ordinary transactions could have hidden dangers. Trust and kindness were valuable, but they could also be exploited. Tommy learned to be more cautious, more aware of the potential risks lurking behind friendly faces and seemingly harmless requests. The Gift Card Scam became a turning point in Tommy's life, a lesson in skepticism and vigilance that would shape his approach to work, relationships, and life itself.

Story 22: he Scholarship Swindle

Maria, an ambitious and bright 18-year-old, had big dreams. College was on the horizon, and she was determined to study at a prestigious university, majoring in environmental science. However, she knew that the tuition fees would be a significant burden on her family. So, she dedicated herself to applying for scholarships, scouring websites, and filling out applications late into the night.

One day, she came across an advertisement for a scholarship that seemed too good to be true. The "Future Leaders of Tomorrow" scholarship promised full tuition coverage, including room and board, for deserving students demonstrating leadership skills. Maria's heart raced. It was the perfect opportunity, exactly what she needed. She clicked on the link and found a professionally designed website filled with testimonials from previous winners, pictures of happy students on campuses, and an easy-to-fill-out application form.

The only catch was a small application fee of $50, explained as a processing charge. Maria hesitated but concluded that it was a small price to pay for such a life-changing opportunity. She filled out the application, paid the fee, and waited anxiously for a response.

Weeks turned into months, and Maria heard nothing. She tried contacting the organization through the email provided on their website but received no reply. Doubt began to creep in, and a nagging feeling of unease settled in her stomach.

Eventually, she decided to do more research and discovered online forums filled with other students who had applied for the same scholarship and faced the same silence.

The realization hit her like a ton of bricks: she had been scammed. The "Future Leaders of Tomorrow" scholarship was a fraud, a carefully crafted scheme to prey on hopeful students like Maria. Her dreams were shattered, and the $50 fee, though not a huge sum, felt like a slap in the face.

The experience was a painful one, filled with disappointment and self-reproach. Maria felt foolish, tricked by her own optimism and trust. But as the weeks went by, she chose to learn from the experience rather than dwell on the loss. She became more vigilant, verifying the legitimacy of scholarships and warning others about the scam she had encountered.

Her determination to succeed remained unbroken, and she continued to pursue her dream of higher education, albeit with a more skeptical eye and a hardened resolve.

The Scholarship Swindle served as a painful lesson in the world of financial fraud, a world where even the most promising opportunities could hide a trap. It was a lesson Maria would carry with her into adulthood, a reminder that caution and diligence were essential in pursuing her dreams.

Story 23: The Game of Deception

Jared, a 14-year-old gaming enthusiast, lived for the virtual worlds he explored with his friends. The camaraderie, competition, and sense of accomplishment kept him glued to his computer. He was part of a tight-knit online gaming community, where friendships were forged over shared quests and epic battles.

One day, a new player named "ShadowMaster" joined Jared's favorite game. He was charismatic and skilled, quickly earning respect and admiration within the community. Jared and ShadowMaster hit it off, spending hours playing together and chatting about their lives outside the game.

ShadowMaster claimed to be a game developer working on a new and groundbreaking project. He painted vivid pictures of a virtual world unlike anything they'd ever seen, filled with adventure, intrigue, and innovation. Jared was fascinated and felt privileged to be privy to such exciting insider information.

As their friendship deepened, ShadowMaster began to share more details about his project, expressing a desire to include Jared in the beta testing phase. All he needed, he explained, was some assistance with funding to finalize the development.

Jared was hesitant but entranced by the idea of being part of something big. ShadowMaster's stories were compelling, and his enthusiasm was contagious. After much consideration, Jared decided to invest some of his savings, believing that he was supporting a friend and a dream.

They arranged the transfer, and Jared felt a thrill of excitement as he imagined himself exploring the new game, a pioneer in a virtual frontier.

Weeks passed, and ShadowMaster's presence in the game began to wane. Jared's inquiries about the project were met with vague responses and promises of updates "soon."

The excitement began to turn into doubt, and Jared's intuition told him that something was amiss. Eventually, ShadowMaster disappeared altogether, leaving Jared with a sinking feeling and a growing sense of betrayal. The truth became inescapable: he had been scammed.

Jared's trust had been exploited, his friendship with ShadowMaster revealed as nothing more than a manipulative game of deception. The loss of money was painful, but the loss of trust was even more devastating. He reported the incident to the game's administrators and shared his story with his friends, warning them about the dangers of trusting strangers online.

His experience became a somber lesson for the entire community, a stark reminder that even in a virtual world, real-world consequences could be lurking around the corner. The Game of Deception left Jared wiser but more guarded, a young gamer who had learned the hard way that not all players play fair.

Story 24: The Mirage of Easy Wealth

Yasir, a 16-year-old high school student, was known for his entrepreneurial spirit. He often found creative ways to earn money, from selling homemade snacks to offering tutoring services. His friends admired his drive, and his family encouraged his ambitions.

One day, Yasir stumbled upon an online advertisement that promised quick and substantial profits through currency trading. The advertisement led to a website with testimonials from young people claiming to have made significant money in a short amount of time.

It was called "Al-Malik Trading Academy," and it offered courses and mentorship to aspiring traders. Yasir's curiosity was piqued. The idea of earning money through trading appealed to his entrepreneurial nature, and he found himself drawn to the promises of wealth and success.

He signed up for a free webinar and was impressed by the

charismatic presenter, Tarek, who claimed to be a self-made millionaire through currency trading. Tarek's confidence and success stories were captivating, and Yasir felt a growing excitement about the possibilities.

At the end of the webinar, Tarek offered a special training package, including exclusive access to his trading strategies and personal mentorship, all for a "limited time" price. Yasir hesitated, the cost was significant, but the potential rewards seemed even greater.

After much contemplation, he decided to invest in the program, using his hard-earned savings.

He believed in himself and saw this as an opportunity to take his financial journey to the next level. The courses were engaging at first, filled with jargon and complex charts. Yasir felt a sense of importance as he delved into the world of trading. Tarek was always available, guiding him through the lessons and encouraging him to invest real money in the market.

Yasir began to trade, following Tarek's advice and strategies. But the profits he had anticipated were elusive. Losses started to mount, and Yasir's excitement turned into anxiety. Doubts crept in, and Yasir began to question the legitimacy of Al-Malik Trading Academy. He reached out to other students and found similar stories of loss and disillusionment. The truth became painfully clear: Tarek's academy was a mirage, a carefully constructed illusion designed to lure aspiring traders into parting with their money. Tarek's strategies were flawed, his success stories fabricated, and his promises empty.

Yasir felt a deep sense of betrayal and anger. His entrepreneurial spirit had been exploited, and his trust shattered. He reported to the academy and shared his experience with others, hoping to prevent them from falling into the same trap. The Mirage of Easy Wealth became a defining moment in Yasir's life, a harsh lesson in skepticism and discernment. He realized that true success required more than promises and shortcuts; it required hard work, integrity, and a willingness to learn from mistakes.

Story 25: Nadia's Stolen Identity

Nadia, a 17-year-old high school student from Amman, was known for her academic excellence and dedication to her studies. Her friends often sought her advice on various subjects, especially when it came to technology and the internet.

One day, Nadia received an email claiming to be from a popular social media platform, stating that her account had been compromised. The email looked official, complete with the company's logo and formatting. It instructed her to click on a link to verify her account and reset her password.

Nadia was alarmed and acted quickly, clicking on the link and following the instructions. She thought she was taking the right steps to protect her account, but something didn't feel quite right. A few days later, Nadia's friends began to receive strange messages from her social media account, promoting products and sharing links to dubious websites. Nadia was horrified and quickly realized that her account had been hacked.

What she initially believed to be a legitimate email was, in fact, a phishing attempt by cybercriminals. By clicking on the link and providing her credentials, she had unknowingly handed over control of her account. The realization was a shock to Nadia, who prided herself on her technological savvy. She felt violated and angry, knowing that her identity had been stolen and misused.

She took immediate action, reporting the incident to the platform's support team and working to regain control of her account. She also reached out to her friends, warning them about the scam and urging them to be cautious with suspicious links.

Despite her efforts, the damage was done. Her trust in online security was shaken, and the experience left her feeling vulnerable and exposed. Nadia's Stolen Identity became a turning point in her life, prompting her to learn more about cybersecurity and online safety. She began to share her knowledge with others, conducting workshops at her school and becoming an advocate for responsible internet use. She understood that the internet's vast and interconnected landscape was filled with both opportunities and risks.

Her experience served as a reminder that vigilance and awareness were essential in navigating the digital world, where a single click could have far-reaching consequences.

Story 26: Sami's Illusionary Friendship

Sami, a 15-year-old boy from a small town in Jordan, was an introverted teenager with a passion for art and music. He often found solace in online communities where he could connect with like-minded individuals. In one of the online forums, he met Lina, who shared his interests and seemed to understand his world. They quickly became virtual friends, chatting daily, sharing their artworks, and discussing their favorite bands.

Lina was warm and empathetic, providing Sami with a sense of connection and belonging that he hadn't felt before. Their friendship blossomed, and Sami found himself opening up, sharing personal details and even his family's financial struggles. After several months, Lina confided in Sami about a lucrative investment opportunity. She explained that her uncle was involved in an art trading business and was looking for small investors to expand the operation. The returns promised to be substantial, and Lina's excitement was contagious.

Sami was hesitant but trusted Lina implicitly. The idea of helping his family financially and making something of his passion for art was too enticing to resist. He gathered his savings and sent them to Lina's uncle's account, believing that he was making a wise investment. Lina thanked him profusely, assuring him that he had made a great decision.

Weeks turned into months, and the promised returns never

materialized. Sami's inquiries were met with excuses and delays. The warm and friendly Lina became distant, and her messages were filled with vague promises. Eventually, Lina stopped responding altogether, and Sami was left with a sinking feeling of betrayal. He realized that he had been deceived, that the friendship and the investment were nothing but an elaborate scam.

Sami's Illusionary Friendship shattered his trust in online connections and left him feeling foolish and vulnerable. The loss of money was painful, but the loss of a friend was devastating. He learned a painful lesson about trust and the potential dangers of online relationships. He became more guarded and cautious, understanding that the virtual world could be as complex and deceptive as the real one. And his experience served as a cautionary tale, a reminder that not all friendships are genuine, and that skepticism and discernment are essential in the age of digital connections.

Story 27: Omar's Costly Lesson in Online Shopping

Omar, a 16-year-old teenager from Zarqa, was eagerly saving up for a new smartphone. He had his eyes on a particular model, and every dinar he earned from his part-time job brought him closer to his goal.

One day, while browsing through an online marketplace, he stumbled upon a deal that seemed too good to be true. A seller was offering the exact smartphone he wanted at a fraction of the retail price. The description was detailed, the pictures were clear, and the seller had a few positive reviews.

Omar was thrilled and quickly contacted the seller; a man named Faisal. Faisal explained that he had bought the phones in bulk for his business and was selling the extras at a discount. His story seemed plausible, and Omar's excitement overpowered any reservations he might have had. After a brief exchange of messages, Omar transferred the money to Faisal's account and waited eagerly for his new phone. Days turned into weeks, and the smartphone never arrived.

Omar's messages to Faisal went unanswered, and soon the seller's profile disappeared from the online marketplace altogether.

Omar was crushed. He realized that he had fallen victim to an online shopping scam, and his hard-earned savings were gone. The dream of owning the new smartphone was shattered, and he felt a mixture of anger, embarrassment, and disbelief.

He reported the incident to the website's administrators and learned that Faisal's positive reviews were fake, part of a pattern of deception used to lure unsuspecting buyers.

Omar's Costly Lesson in Online Shopping became a defining experience in his young life. He understood that the excitement of a good deal could cloud judgment and that caution and critical thinking were essential in navigating the online marketplace.

He shared his story with his friends and family, turning his loss into a lesson for others. He also became more vigilant and discerning in his online purchases, recognizing that not all bargains are genuine, and that trust must be earned, not assumed.

Omar's experience served as a reminder that the allure of convenience and discounts online can sometimes hide pitfalls and dangers, and that wisdom and caution are invaluable tools in the digital age.

Story 28: Aiko's Dream Scholarship: A Deception Unveiled

Aiko, a 17-year-old girl living in a bustling city, was a dedicated student with dreams of studying abroad. Her parents, Yumi and Hiroshi, supported her ambitions, but they knew that financing her education in a foreign country would be a challenge.

One day, Aiko stumbled upon an advertisement for a scholarship program that seemed tailor-made for her. It was the "Bright Future Scholars," a program supposedly designed to support talented students from Asia in pursuing their education in prestigious universities abroad.

Thrilled by the opportunity, Aiko clicked on the link and found a professional-looking website filled with success stories, testimonials, and detailed information about the scholarship. She felt a surge of hope and excitement.

The application process was thorough, requiring personal information, academic records, and even a video submission detailing her dreams and aspirations. Aiko worked tirelessly on her application, pouring her heart and soul into every detail.

After submitting her application, she received an email from a woman named Mei, who introduced herself as the scholarship coordinator. Mei was encouraging and supportive, guiding Aiko through the next stages of the process.

Aiko was eventually informed that she was one of the finalists and that a small administrative fee was required to complete the process. The amount seemed insignificant compared to the value of the scholarship, and Mei's reassurances quelled any doubts.

With her parents' blessing, Aiko paid the fee and waited for the confirmation of her scholarship award. Days turned into weeks, and despite Mei's promises, there were no updates.

Concerned, Aiko began to investigate further and discovered that the website, testimonials, and even Mei's identity were all fabricated. The "Bright Future Scholars" program was a sham, a sophisticated scam preying on the dreams and aspirations of young students like her.

Aiko's Dream Scholarship had been a deception, and the realization was a crushing blow. She felt humiliated and betrayed, her dreams momentarily derailed by the cruel illusion.

But Aiko's spirit was resilient. She reported the scam, shared her story, and used the experience as a catalyst to strengthen her resolve. She continued to pursue her dreams, understanding that setbacks and deceit were obstacles to be overcome, not defining failures.

Her experience served as a powerful lesson in trust and discernment, a reminder that appearances can be deceiving, and that vigilance, research, and critical thinking are essential in pursuing opportunities, especially in the complex and interconnected digital world.

Story 29: Min-Jun's Gaming Misadventure

Min-Jun, a 14-year-old boy from Seoul, was an avid gamer. He spent hours playing his favorite online games with friends, always seeking new challenges and adventures.

One day, while browsing through a gaming forum, he came across an advertisement for an exclusive in-game item. The item was rare and would give him a significant advantage in his favorite game. It was being sold by a user named Ji-Hoon, who had several positive reviews from other forum members.

Excited by the opportunity, Min-Jun contacted Ji-Hoon, who seemed friendly and knowledgeable. They negotiated a price, and Ji-Hoon instructed Min-Jun to pay using a specific online payment platform.

Min-Jun hesitated momentarily but was swayed by Ji-Hoon's reputation on the forum and the allure of the rare item. He transferred the money, trusting that Ji-Hoon would deliver as promised.

Days went by, and the in-game item never appeared. Min-Jun's messages to Ji-Hoon were met with excuses and delays, and soon Ji-Hoon stopped responding altogether.

Frustrated and confused, Min-Jun realized that he had been scammed. The positive reviews and friendly demeanor had been a façade, a carefully crafted deception to lure him into a false sense of security.

Min-Jun's Gaming Misadventure was a harsh and

unexpected lesson. He had believed that his knowledge of the gaming world and the community had made him immune to such deceit.

But he had underestimated the cunning of those who sought to exploit the passion and trust of gamers like him.

He reported the incident to the forum administrators and shared his experience with his friends, turning his loss into a warning for others.

He understood that trust must be earned, and that caution and critical thinking were essential even in the seemingly safe spaces of his beloved gaming world.

His experience served as a reminder that scams and deception can infiltrate even the most familiar and cherished aspects of our lives, and that vigilance and discernment are essential tools in recognizing and avoiding the traps set by those who seek to exploit our trust and enthusiasm.

Story 30: Anastasia's Deceptive Tutor

Anastasia, a 16-year-old student from St. Petersburg, was struggling with her mathematics subject. Her parents, worried about her falling grades, decided to look for an online tutor to help her improve.

They came across a website promoting a highly qualified tutor named Dmitri, who specialized in teaching mathematics to teenagers. Dmitri's profile was impressive, filled with credentials, certifications, and glowing testimonials from satisfied parents and students.

Anastasia's parents contacted Dmitri, who was eloquent and reassuring. He explained his teaching methodology, offered a personalized study plan, and even provided a free initial consultation to assess Anastasia's needs.

Everything seemed perfect, and Anastasia's parents were relieved to have found such a professional and dedicated tutor. They agreed on the fee and paid for a month's worth of lessons in advance.

Dmitri started the lessons with Anastasia, who found his teaching style engaging and helpful. For the first week, everything went smoothly, and Anastasia's confidence began to grow.

But after the first week, Dmitri's behavior changed. He started missing sessions, arriving late, and seemed unprepared. His explanations became vague, and the quality of his teaching declined rapidly.

Anastasia's parents reached out to Dmitri, expressing their concerns, but were met with excuses and promises that went unfulfilled.

Growing suspicious, they began to investigate Dmitri's credentials and discovered that many of his qualifications were fabricated, and some of the testimonials were fake.

They realized that Dmitri's initial professionalism and competence had been a calculated deception to gain their trust and money.

Anastasia's Deceptive Tutor had been a clever scam, exploiting the vulnerability and desperation of parents and students seeking academic help.

They reported Dmitri to the authorities and sought to warn others about his deceitful practices. Anastasia's experience with the deceptive tutor became a cautionary tale, a stark reminder that even the most professional-looking profiles could hide a scammer's true intentions.

The experience taught Anastasia and her parents to be more vigilant and discerning in their online interactions, understanding that trust must be verified, and that appearances can be deceiving.

Story 31: Lucy's Unexpected Encounter with Identity Theft

Lucy, a 15-year-old girl from a small town in the United States, was a typical teenager with a passion for social media. She enjoyed sharing her life, interests, and hobbies with her online friends.

One day, she received a friend request from a person named Michael, who shared several common interests and had mutual friends. His profile seemed genuine, and Lucy accepted the request without much thought.

Over time, Michael became an active participant in Lucy's online world, liking her posts, leaving friendly comments, and occasionally chatting with her through private messages. Lucy felt a connection and trusted Michael as one of her online friends.

Months went by, and Lucy started noticing strange activities on her social media accounts. Some of her private information, including photos and personal details, were appearing on other websites. She received mysterious emails and even unsolicited phone calls.

Terrified and confused, Lucy sought help from her parents, who contacted the authorities. An investigation revealed that Michael was not who he claimed to be. His profile was a façade, carefully crafted to gain Lucy's trust and access her personal information.

Lucy's Unexpected Encounter with Identity Theft had been a slow and insidious process, a deception that exploited her trust and openness. The person behind Michael's profile had used the information Lucy shared online to steal her identity, creating fake accounts and engaging in fraudulent activities in her name. The experience was a traumatic and eye-opening lesson for Lucy. She realized that her online world was not as safe as she had believed, and that her trust had made her vulnerable to those who would exploit it. With the support of her family and authorities, Lucy took steps to reclaim her online identity, tightening her security settings, and becoming more cautious about sharing personal information.

Lucy's experience served as a sobering reminder that even seemingly innocent online friendships could have hidden dangers, and that vigilance, caution, and critical thinking are essential in navigating the complex and interconnected digital landscape.

Story 32: Emily's Unintended Consequence: A Donation Gone Wrong

Emily, an 18-year-old girl from a close-knit community, was known for her kind heart and willingness to help others. She believed in the power of compassion and often contributed to various causes that resonated with her values.

One day, while strolling through social media, Emily came across a heart-wrenching story about a war-torn region in desperate need of humanitarian aid. The story was accompanied by an appeal from a charity organization named "XYZ" that claimed to provide food, shelter, and medical support to the victims of the conflict. Moved by the plight of the people in the images, Emily felt a strong urge to help. The organization's website was filled with touching testimonials, pictures of volunteers at work, and detailed explanations of their mission and impact.

Everything about "XYZ" seemed genuine and aligned with Emily's desire to make a difference. Without hesitation, she clicked on the donation link and contributed what she could, feeling a sense of pride and fulfillment in her decision. Weeks went by, and Emily continued to follow "XYZ," feeling connected to a cause that mattered deeply to her. However, one day, a news story broke that sent shockwaves through Emily's world. "XYZ" had been exposed as a front for a terrorist organization, funneling donations from well-meaning individuals to finance their nefarious activities. The realization that her innocent donation had been used to support something so abhorrent was a crushing blow to Emily. She felt betrayed, confused, and overwhelmed by guilt, even though she had acted with the purest of intentions.

Emily's Unintended Consequence: A Donation Gone Wrong was a painful lesson in the complexity and hidden dangers of charitable giving. Her desire to help had been exploited by those who understood how to manipulate empathy and trust. With the support of her family and community, Emily took steps to report her experience and learn from it. She understood that her intentions had been noble, but that caution, and due diligence were necessary to ensure that her contributions reached those truly in need. Her experience became a catalyst for awareness and education, both for herself and others in her community. She realized that goodwill alone was not enough, that discernment, research, and vigilance were essential in navigating the world of charitable giving, especially in an age where appearances can be so deceiving. Emily's story serves as a stark reminder that even the most well-intended actions can have unintended consequences, and that we must be mindful and discerning in our efforts to contribute positively to the world.

Story 33: Max's Dangerous Gamble: A Teenager Ensnared in a Money Laundering Web

Max, a 17-year-old from a bustling city, was a bright and ambitious teenager. But his ambition, coupled with a desire for easy money, led him down a dangerous path.

While browsing an online forum, Max stumbled upon an offer that seemed too good to be true. A user named "ShadowBroker" was looking for individuals to participate in what was described as a "financial redistribution" scheme. Intrigued, Max engaged in a private conversation with ShadowBroker, who explained the opportunity in more detail.

ShadowBroker promised Max substantial commissions in return for moving money between various bank accounts. Though Max knew deep down that the offer was illegal, the allure of quick cash overpowered his better judgment.

Max's role as a money mule began simply. He would receive funds in his bank account, then transfer them to another account as instructed, keeping a percentage for himself. The transactions were swift and seemingly effortless, and Max quickly became intoxicated by the ease of his new-found income. For several months, Max continued his involvement with ShadowBroker, who praised him for his reliability and efficiency.

Max's confidence grew, and he began to believe that he was invincible, that he had found a loophole that allowed him to profit without consequences. But as with most criminal activities, Max's dangerous gamble eventually caught up with him. A series of transactions drew the attention of law enforcement, and an investigation was launched. Max's life quickly unraveled as the authorities closed in. They were able to trace the transactions back to a larger money laundering operation, with Max serving as a critical link in the chain.

Max was arrested, and the full weight of his actions began to sink in. He realized that his involvement had not only financed criminal organizations but also had severe legal implications for himself.

The trial was swift, and the evidence against Max was overwhelming. He was found guilty of being complicit in a money laundering scheme, and his dreams of wealth and success were shattered as he faced the reality of legal penalties, including fines and possible imprisonment.

Max's Dangerous Gamble serves as a cautionary tale for teenagers who might be tempted by the allure of easy money, without fully understanding the risks and consequences. His story emphasizes the importance of ethics, integrity, and the recognition that illegal shortcuts can lead to devastating ends. The story also highlights the sophisticated nature of financial crimes, where even a seemingly small and insignificant role can contribute to a broader and more harmful criminal enterprise.

FINAL MESSAGE

Financial crimes are like quicksand, pulling us into a murky world where right and wrong often get muddled. They're not just about money—these actions wreck the trust we place in businesses, governments, and even each other. We're talking about age-old shenanigans like fraud, but also new-age trickeries supercharged by technology. And let me tell you, these aren't simple board games; these crimes are complex puzzles involving multiple countries and currencies, like a thriller movie, but with real stakes.

Why should you, as teens, care? Because you guys are more than just the next generation; you're the now generation. You bring an electric blend of creativity, energy, and fresh perspectives to the table. Your age isn't a limitation; it's a superpower. Your voice can amplify the issues we face today and turn them into calls to action. Financial crimes are no different.

But hey, being a teen isn't all about adventures and first loves; it's also a confusing time. You're stepping into adulthood, and that means wanting space and freedom, sometimes without Mom and Dad peeking over your shoulder. It's that exact curiosity and quest for independence that can sometimes put you in the crosshairs of people with bad intentions. Cybercriminals, scam artists, and fraudsters see you not as victims but as opportunities—easy prey they can manipulate for their own gain. Your natural urge for independence, your immersion in the digital world, and even your fearless trust in people can sometimes blind you to risks.

So, what's the fix? First off, keep those lines of communication open. Your parents might not get the latest TikTok trends, but they've seen their share of life's curveballs. Pair your tech-savviness with their life experience to create an unbeatable team. Be aware that criminals are like puppeteers, pulling on your emotional strings to make you do what they want. Whether it's pressure from your friends to make quick cash online or a text message scam asking for your bank details, always think twice.

You live in a world that's advancing at warp speed, and you're not just on the ride—you're co-piloting it. With that role comes responsibility. Your quick wit and adaptability are your shields and swords in the battle against financial crimes. Every decision you make, from being a responsible digital citizen to perhaps diving into a career that fights financial crime, chips away at the mountain of issues we face.

Your fight is our fight. And remember, change isn't reserved for the adults or the experts—it starts with you, here and now. So go out there and be the change-makers, the problem-solvers, and the heroes in your own epic story. Show the world that when it comes to making a difference, age is just a number, but courage is timeless.

The End...